Learning from the Lives of Amazing People

by
Janice Gudeman

illustrated by Kathryn Hyndman

Cover by Kathryn Hyndman

Copyright © Good Apple, Inc., 1988

ISBN No. 0-86653-446-6

Printing No. 98765432

Good Apple, Inc.
Box 299
Carthage, IL 62321-0299

The purchase of this book entitles the buyer to reproduce student activity pages for classroom use only. Any other use requires written permission from Good Apple, Inc.

All rights reserved. Printed in the United States of America.

FOREWORD

Biographies have always been my favorite form of reading, because here life is not abstract but very real. All of the people included in this book have had to overcome difficulties and disappointments. They've been frustrated by setbacks and failures—but in each case they used it as an opportunity to learn more about themselves and life. In my own life people like these have been beacons of hope and living models of courage.

Janice Gudeman has done something very special in her book *Learning from the Lives of Amazing People*. She has not only brought these people to life in a very rich way for students of all ages to enjoy, but she has also created ways through which students can have a genuine **encounter** with their heroes. It's a stroke of genius. This book is not only inspirational but practical.

Through these encounters young people will actually have an opportunity to develop the very attitudes, skills and values that they admire so much in the man or woman they're reading about. This is a book to be treasured—by teachers, parents, and mostly the students themselves—because they will actually *participate* in the making of this book. Therefore, the impact of these lives on them will be even more powerful.

Our children *are* our future. We must do everything we can to prepare them for the most complex future anyone has had to face. What better way than to provide for them *Learning from the Lives of Amazing People*.

Tim Hansel
Founder and President of
Summit Expedition, Inc.

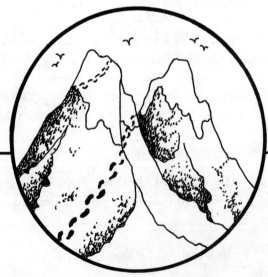

DEDICATION

This book is lovingly dedicated to my mother and in memory of my father. Their lives have exemplified the meaning of love, commitment, courage, and perseverance. My dad's battle with cancer taught many how to live and stirred the inspiration and ideas for this book. My father's footprints are planted in my heart, and may his legacy of love and wisdom live on through this book and touch the hearts of many.

ACKNOWLEDGMENTS

This book is a labor of love about people and a gift of encouragement to people. The lives of people whose paths I have crossed are reflected in this book. My experience with people in my life are intricately interwoven in these pages. The influence of other people have made a lasting impact on my life and writing. Therefore, this book is a bouquet of gratitude to these special people.

My parents, my sister Bev, her husband Bill and family, and my brother Darrel and his wife Karen are pillars of strength and love, upholding me in my endeavors. I express my deep appreciation to my parents, family, relatives, and friends for their love and encouragement in walking through the adventures and adversities in my own life.

I am thankful to Tim Hansel for writing the foreword.

I extend my sincere appreciation to Jill Kinmont Boothe, Marva Collins, Stan Cottrell, Robin Graham, Sally Haddock, Tim Hansel, Carolyn Koons, Art Linkletter, Cynthia Rowland McClure, Josh McDowell, Paul Meier, Pat Moore, Harold Morris, Dale Evans Rogers, Gale Sayers, June Scobee, and Tom Sullivan for being a part of this book. What an adventure it has been to walk in the footsteps of these amazing people and write this book. It has been a life-changing experience.

I would like to express gratitude to Jill Kinmont Boothe and Pat Moore for sharing their artwork in this book.

I thank Mary Crowley's daughter and son, Ruth Shanahan and Don Carter; Eric Liddell's sister, Jenny Somerville; and S. Rickly Christian of Focus on the Family Publishing for their help.

I am grateful to Don Hawkins, Clinic Director, and Vicky Warren, Executive Secretary of the Minirth-Meier Clinic, a counseling center in Richardson, a Dallas suburb, for reading the manuscript of this book.

Special thanks go to the amazing people of Good Apple: Gary Grimm, Jill Eckhardt, Virginia Allison, Opal Jackson, and Kathryn Hyndman. Their sensitivity, insight, creative skills, and expertise have made my adventure with writing a positive and challenging experience.

I wish to thank Nancy Berry, a friend and a teacher, for her poem.

My hope is that you will be challenged and encouraged, as you walk in the footsteps of these amazing people. May their footprints be planted in your heart, and may your footsteps find new paths of adventure and joy.

TABLE OF CONTENTS

Footsteps in Life's Classroom

Someone in my class is laughing—
Today I shall laugh with him.
Someone else is crying,
Though you will never see a tear;
Today I will speak gently.
There is one who needs understanding,
For he is always misunderstood—
Especially to him I shall listen.
Someone here is angry—
Today I will be known as a blessed peacemaker.
Someone is having a difficult time;
Thoughts of failure cross his mind—
Today I will inspire him to succeed at a task
Ever so small . . . .
Another has been forgotten.
It is easy to do, for there are so many;
But today I must remember to praise him.

I shall trudge home wearily
At the end of the day,
But my footsteps will move
Ever so lightly,
As I dwell upon those mentors before me . . . .
And I shall rejoice in the knowledge
That tomorrow—
I must do all of this again.
I,
You see,
Am a teacher . . . .

Nancy Berry

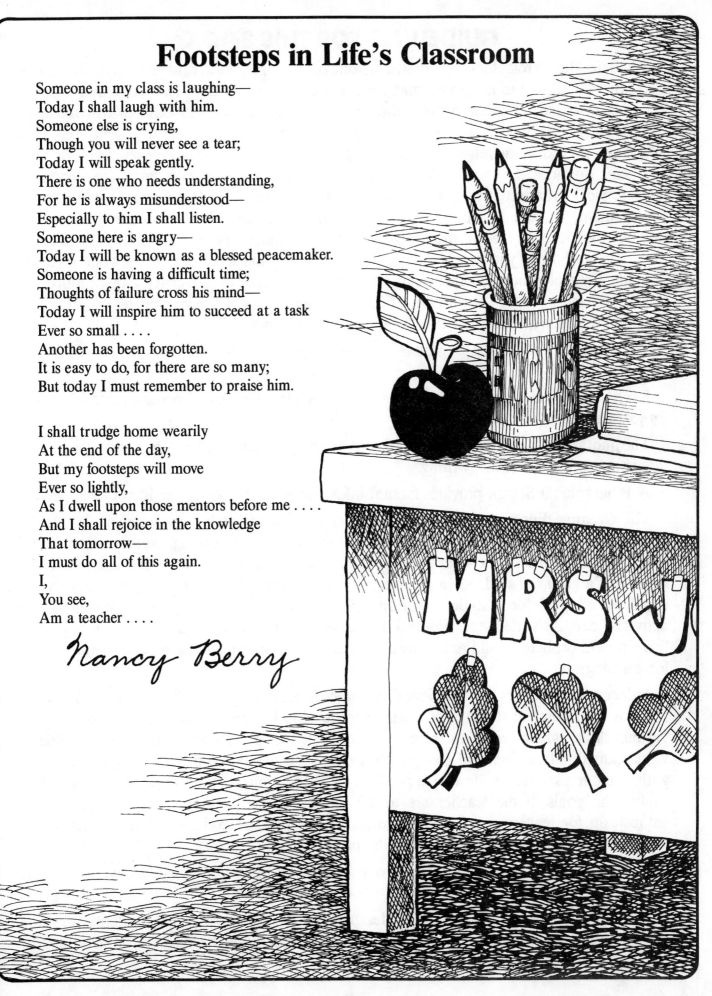

GUIDELINES FOR THIS BOOK

Walk in the heroic footsteps of these amazing people, and find encouragement and inspiration. Follow the footprints that lead to paths of adventure, challenge and insights. Become a student of other people. Each of these people hurdled obstacles in the road of life. These role models are persevering personalities, who have lived adventurous lives and have overcome adversity. Walk through their successes and failures, explore their character qualities, and touch their joys and sorrows. Identify with their experiences to learn to work creatively through problems and build goals for personal growth in academic achievement, as well as character development. Their commitment, determination, and perseverance in each step of the journey led these amazing people to fulfill their dreams. You can, too! How you respond to adversity can be the key to shaping your own life and the lives of others. In the sands of time, the deserts of adversity can produce the growth needed to fulfill your dreams. Follow the footprints of these amazing people, plant them in your heart, and create new footprints of your own.

The format of this book is similar to *Creative Encounters with Creative People* by the same author.

Each unit includes quotations, a Biographical Sketch, Creative Encounters, Independent Projects, and Resource Books.

The quotations and poems in this book can be analyzed and used as topics for inspirational discussions and/or creative writing.

A Biographical Sketch provides factual information to introduce the life of each person.

The Creative Encounters offer opportunities of enrichment for open-ended discussions, brainstorming, researching, creative problem solving, creative writing, creative drama, and hands-on experiences. The Creative Encounters are a variety of activities designed to be used with a group of students in a teacher-directed setting. However, many of the activities could be adapted for a student working alone. The written and oral expression of the activities can be varied and adapted to fit the needs and interests of your group. The learning atmosphere should reflect warmth, care, empathy, encouragement and enthusiasm for learning.

Independent Projects provide ideas for independent study to enhance higher levels of thinking. Independent study helps students to develop self-motivation, self-confidence, and various skills, which will help them to continue learning throughout their lives. Students work individually or in small groups. They select a topic, develop the questions, set goals, gather resources, research, develop a product, share the project, and evaluate the independent study. The goals of the teacher are to act as a resource person, provide guidance and enthusiasm for learning, and encourage quality work. The contract for the independent projects is included as a format to plan the projects. (See page vii.)

The Resource Books provide a variety of references for the activities in Creative Encounters and Independent Projects to aid in the study of each person.

A certificate of commendation is designed to praise and reward students for their outstanding achievements and successes as they journey into the pages of *Learning from the Lives of Amazing People.*

MY INDEPENDENT PROJECT

Title: _____

A brief explanation of my project: _____

_____

Some questions I want to answer: _____

_____

_____

Materials needed: _____

_____

_____

Resources (books, encyclopedias, people, and others): _____

_____

_____

Ideas for sharing my project: _____

_____

_____

Estimation of time needed to complete my project: _____

_____

Date started: _____

Date completed: _____

Steps I will take:

Step 1 _____

Step 2 _____

Step 3 _____

Step 4 _____

Step 5 _____

_____   _____
Teacher's Signature   Student's Signature

CERTIFICATE OF COMMENDATION

Learning from the Lives of Amazing People

This honor is awarded to

_____

for excellence in character development, creative problem solving,
and academic achievement.

Signature _____

Date _____

WALK FROM TRAGEDY TO TRIUMPH

JILL KINMONT BOOTHE

"I want to share some of my experiences with you. My childhood, the fierce desire to compete athletically, the new unexpected challenges during early adulthood, the barriers that for some puzzling reason kept looming up, and finally, new adventures. I'm not sure all this had to do with courage, but I do have this urge to persist.

"My mom and dad had an incredible ability to provide an environment which would enable us to accomplish just about anything my brothers and I set out to do. I have a family who were totally supportive, and they had an uncanny way of seeming not to be sacrificing during many years of great sacrifice. My family has a great sense of humor, and my incredibly cheery, energetic, understanding mother helped enormously. All of this made handling my new state of affairs a little easier."

Jill Kinmont Boothe

BIOGRAPHICAL SKETCH

Growing up, Jill spent most of her time out-of-doors, fishing, horseback riding, hiking, ice-skating, and skiing. Jill and her friend Audro Jo were rodeo fans. They both had summer jobs at the Rocking K Guest Ranch owned by Jill's family in Bishop, California. Jill gave Red Cross swimming lessons for five-year-olds at the public pool. It was sad for Jill when Audro Jo, her friend that she worked, played, and laughed with for four years, was diagnosed with poliomyelitis and went into an iron lung.

During the summers Jill launched herself on a dry-land training program for skiing—a routine of special exercises, one-legged knee bends, cross-country running, and "slalom" practice (hopping back and forth into old automobile tires laid flat on the ground). At Mammoth Mountain, Jill schussed everything she could find. She clocked herself at 55 miles an hour, and some of her runs were undoubtedly faster than that.

Jill and her brother Bob won or placed in race after race. In 1954, at the age of eighteen, Jill was women's amateur slalom champion of the United States. Jill was described in the press as a "new star" and a "glamorous young champion."

Jill's dream was to go to the Olympics. She was a leading candidate for the U.S. Olympic team, and she was competing in the annual Snow Cup giant slalom in the mountains east of Salt Lake City in 1955. In this last qualifying race before the Olympic tryouts, she crashed onto the snow at forty miles an hour. She slid and spun, and in the middle of the final tumble Jill felt within her body a sudden dull vibration. She broke her neck, and since then she has been a quadriplegic, paralyzed from the shoulders down. As a spectator, Jill did attend the 1956 Winter Olympic Games that she had worked so hard to get to as a competitor.

Jill and her husband John live in Bishop, California, in a home with a spectacular view of the Sierras. In 1967 Jill organized a summer reading program for Indian children, while she was still teaching in the Los Angeles area. Jill is a reading specialist, and she is especially talented in motivating children to learn.

Jill had won a fine reputation as the best kind of competitor. The courage and persistence with which she has overcome obstacles have made her one of the most admired figures in international sports. These qualities are also manifested in her career as an aspiring teacher.

CREATIVE ENCOUNTER #1 ....Kaleidoscopes and Turning Points

"When Jill thought about all the things that had altered because of the accident, she was surprised at how gradual most of the changes had been. The one overt physical change had been drastic, of course—from exuberant good health to permanent paralysis in a moment."

Imagine gazing into a kaleidoscope. Focus on the intriguing array of colors and patterns. Twist it now to see another intricate change of colors and patterns. Keep turning it to watch the pieces fit together in new and different patterns.

Think of a turning point in your life; maybe it was a dream shattered into many pieces. Or it could have been a twist of a key that unlocked a door for a dream to come true. Try to fit the pieces together to see the turning point with a new perspective—to create a new dream.

Draw an array of patterns of colorful, geometric designs inside the kaleidoscope to represent the making of something beautiful out of something broken. On another sheet of paper draw a large circle with a point in the center. Write in a circular fashion inside the circle about a turning point and the consequential changes that occurred in your life.

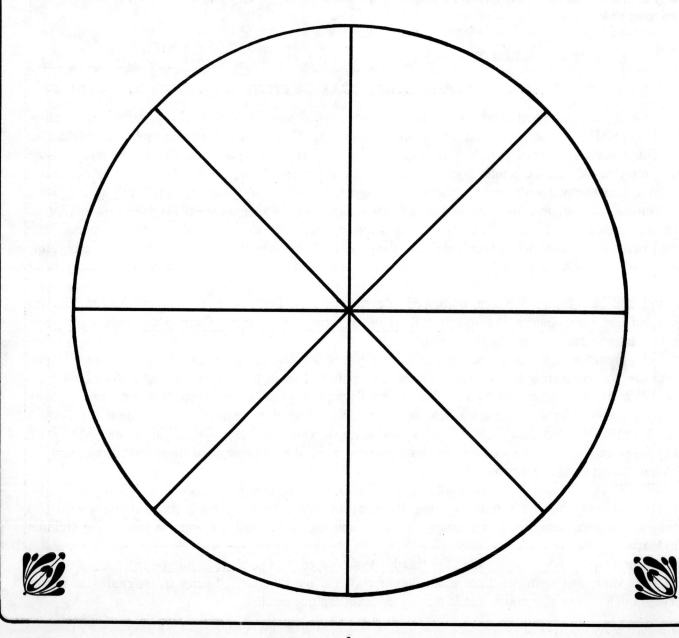

CREATIVE ENCOUNTER #2 ....A Window to the Sky

"Jill remembered what Audra Jo had said about her own misfortune: 'It forced me to grow up.' Jill was grateful that she had been forced to look beyond her small, bright little world of competitive skiing, to notice and begin to care about a broader universe."

Paul Harvey has enthusiastically said, *"Get up when you fall down."* *"The ability to get up after you have fallen or been knocked down is the secret of every achievement,"* states the author of *Where There's a Wall There's a Way.* Imagine you are beginning to learn to ski with Jill as a teenager. You struggle, lose your balance, slip and slide, tumble, and fall. You pick yourself up again and again. You take a break and find comfort in resting near the fireplace at the ski lodge. You look out the window at the breathtaking view of the sky and the snow-covered mountains. Your goal is set before you, and you are ready to get up and try again.

Jill journeyed from triumph to tragedy and back. Turn your troubles into triumphs. Turn your obstacles into opportunities. Open the window to the sky.

In the windows write down a few obstacles in your life. Write about opportunities that opened due to the obstacles. For example, maybe you were cut from the team, but it gave you more time to develop another skill.

OBSTACLES   OPPORTUNITIES

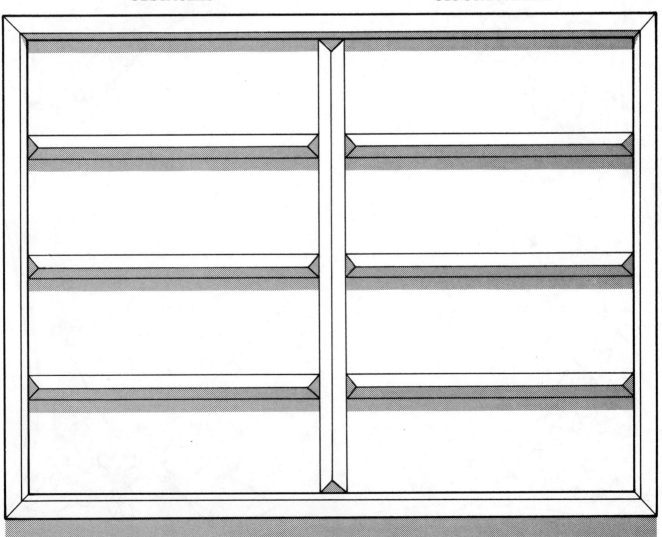

CREATIVE ENCOUNTER #3 .... A Bouquet of Encouragement

Dear Miss Kinmont,

Why are you going to leave? The school will be lost without you. You've been so kind to everyone and you're the nicest person I know. You're our hero and you're the only one we've got.

Peter

Jill received this letter from one of her students when she decided to move. Imagine a cascade of flowers being thrust to the wind. The petals and the fragrance of the flowers spread afar. That is the way encouragement spreads. Your words of encouragement could touch one person, and that person could be inspired to help another and on and on. The far-reaching effect that you have upon people could travel endlessly. Encouragement helps a person to blossom and grow.

Write a genuine letter of encouragement to someone expressing your care and appreciation, sharing their joy, spurring them to go on in spite of difficulties, and/or mentioning admirable character qualities. If desired, give a bouquet of flowers with your bouquet of encouragement.

CREATIVE ENCOUNTER #4 .... Understanding Misunderstanding

A university in California refused to allow Jill to study there, because she couldn't stand in a classroom or walk up and down steps. Her applications to teach in schools were later turned down for the same reason. But Jill persisted. Eventually she earned a teaching certificate at the University of Washington. In 1967 she was hired as a reading specialist in Beverly Hills.

In the above incident Jill experienced the sting of misunderstanding. You have probably experienced in your own little world a measure of what we could call persecution. You didn't mean anything by your words or actions, but they were misread and an offense was created. You may have tried to do what was right, but yet you were falsely accused or treated unjustly.

Describe an experience when you were misunderstood. When were you falsely accused? How could you respond differently the next time you are misunderstood?

Role-play the following situation extemporaneously. Afterwards discuss several alternatives to prevent misunderstanding and to help your friends understand. How could you help them to change? Now role-play the situation again trying a new approach.

Be supportive to someone you know is hurting. Reach out without fear of what others may think or say.

A person new to your class is standing alone near the swings. At recess you hear your friends whispering, making fun of her, because she is different. In fact, she is somewhat handicapped. You hear that your friends have decided not to accept this new person into their group. You look at the new person and perceive she is longing to be accepted. She seems rather shy and quiet.

Your friends could make fun of you for trying to be friends with someone who is different. Yet you empathize with her. You were once new and know how hard it is to start over and make new friends. You want to reach out to her. You take a few steps toward her, and you hear your peers start to whisper about you. You stop and hesitate.

Will you take the steps necessary to reach out to a new, hurting person or succumb to the mocking whispers of your group? Are you willing to be misunderstood to help to understand another?

CREATIVE ENCOUNTER #5 .... Encouraging One Another

The 1956 Olympics was a real possibility if Jill could concentrate on skiing for the next two seasons. She asked her parents, *"Do you think I'm being foolish? I mean, I do want to try, but maybe I haven't got the ability."*

Jill's dad replied, *"Well, you've got plenty of **poss**-ability, honeygirl, and if that's what you want you sure ought to give it a whirl."*

All of us need encouragement. We need someone to believe in us, to reassure and reinforce us, to help us pick up the pieces and go on, and to provide us with increased determination in spite of the odds. Encouragement is the act of inspiring others with renewed courage, spirit, or hope. Just think of the many people who are discouraged and the potential that is lost, because of lack of encouragement. An encouraging smile or comment can make a difference.

Dr. Gene Getz in *Encouraging One Another* suggests the following checklist to help you evaluate yourself in this area. Are you able to get excited about the good things that happen to others? Are you able to tell them that you're glad? Can you enter into their joy? Are you able to accept other people for who they are? Do you see the best in people? Do you freely associate with people who are different from you? If you do, you are an encourager!

Brainstorm ideas that will help spark an interest in putting your encouragment into action. Choose an idea and encourage someone today.

Jill Kinmont Boothe's illustrations on this page and page 7 can be used to add direction to many of the Creative Encounters and Independent Projects suggested in this section.

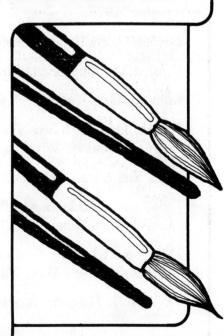

INDEPENDENT PROJECTS—BOOTHE

1. Teaching is fascinating to Jill, and she loves to see children enjoying a book. Read a book about learning to ski or learning another skill. Prepare a lesson plan and teach the class how to learn to ski or another skill.
2. Watercolor painting is Jill's favorite hobby. Using a special brace with clamps, she holds the brush. She mostly paints landscapes. Paint a picture of one of your favorite outdoor scenes or another picture of your choice.
3. Joni Eareckson Tada is a friend of Jill Kinmont Boothe. Joni and Jill both have to borrow others' hands to enable them to be free to share their own unique talents with others. Joni has a recording called *Joni with Joni's Kids—I've Got Wheels!* Joni and Jill are both dependent upon wheels. Make a mobile with things with wheels: a wheelchair, a van, a skateboard, roller skates, etc. Write about Joni and Jill's struggles, needs, and contributions. Summarize what you have learned from Joni and Jill's lives about needing others and reaching out to others.
4. Come ride in a wheelchair. Come walk in braces. Hear with your eyes. Speak with your hands. Think about the needs of the handicapped. Plan and draw a playground that is fun and safe for handicapped children.
5. Bob Wieland lost his legs serving in Vietnam. He took 4,900,016 steps, covering 3,000 miles in his 3½-year walk across America on his hands, raising money to feed the hungry. He is a speaker and lives in Laguna Hills, California. Write an essay about other handicapped people who have attained great heights in sports events or in other pursuits.

RESOURCE BOOKS—BOOTHE

Adams, Barbara. *Like It Is: Facts and Feelings About Handicaps from Kids Who Know.* New York: Walker and Co., 1979.

Crabb, Lawrence J., Jr., and Dan B. Allender. *Encouragement: The Key to Caring.* Grand Rapids, Michigan: Zondervan Publishing House, 1984.

Evans, Harold, Brian Jackman, and Mark Ottaway. *We Learned to Ski.* New York: St. Martin's Press, Inc., 1975.

Hawley, Gloria Hope. *Champions.* Grand Rapids, Michigan: Zondervan Publishing House, 1984.

Henriod, Lorraine. *Special Olympics and Paralympics.* New York: Franklin Watts, 1979.

Killilea, Marie. *Karen.* Englewood Cliffs, New Jersey: Prentice-Hall, Inc., 1952.

Polston, Don H. *Where There's a Wall There's a Way: 14 Proven Ways to Turn Your Obstacles into Opportunities!* Wheaton, Illinois: Tyndale House Publishers, Inc., 1985.

Tada, Joni Eareckson. *Choices—Changes.* Grand Rapids, Michigan: Zondervan Publishing House, 1986.

Tada, Joni Eareckson, and Bev Singleton. *Friendship Unlimited: How You Can Help a Disabled Friend.* Wheaton, Illinois: Harold Shaw Publishing, 1987.

Thompson, Charlotte E. *Raising a Handicapped Child: A Helpful Guide for Parents of the Physically Disabled.* New York: William Morrow and Co., Inc., 1986.

Valens, E.G. *The Other Side of the Mountain.* New York: Warner Books, Inc., 1975.

_____. *The Other Side of the Mountain Part 2.* New York: Warner Books, Inc., 1978.

WALK FROM FAILURE TO SUCCESS

MARVA COLLINS

*"Throughout the year, as in every year of my teaching, my main goal was to motivate the students to make something worthwhile of their lives. Everything we said or did in class was directed toward that aim. More than anything I wanted to supplant apathy and defeatism with positive expectations. I didn't want my children to feel stigmatized by where they lived. I didn't want them to succumb to a ghetto mentality. If I had my way, they would dream and hope and strive and **obtain** success.*

"We have to teach children self-reliance and self-respect. We have to teach them the importance of learning, of developing skills, of doing for themselves. I am always reminding my students that if you give a man a fish, he will eat for only a day. If you teach him how to fish, he will feed himself for a lifetime. That's why I stay in Garfield Park. The legacy I want to leave behind is a generation of children who realize that you can't get something for nothing, who are proud and resourceful enough to take care of their own."

Marva N. Collins

BIOGRAPHICAL SKETCH

Growing up during the Depression, Marva was wealthy, pampered, and sheltered by small-town innocence and a protective father. Her father, a clever businessman, was one of the richest black men in Monroeville, Alabama. It was a happy, carefree childhood. Those were the years that made her what she is.

Marva learned to read before she was old enough to go to school. Along with the other black children, she spent the primary grades at Bethlehem Academy. She graduated from Escambia County Training School and chose Clark College in Atlanta, an exclusive, all-black, liberal arts school for girls.

In June 1959, she left for Chicago and later taught in the Chicago public school system. A group of neighborhood women organizing a community school wanted to start a private elementary school for children in the Garfield Park area. They asked Marva to be director. Meeting in a basement classroom, the new school opened its doors on September 8, 1975. When they changed the location to the vacant upstairs apartment in their house, her husband remodeled the facilities. Their two children, Cindy and Patrick, attended her school.

When a columnist from the *Sun-Times* came to visit her school, he watched *"four-year-olds writing sentences like 'See the physician' and 'Aesop wrote fables' and discussing diphthongs and diacritical marks— calling them correctly by name."* He heard *"second graders reciting passages from Shakespeare, Longfellow and Kipling"* and *"third graders learning about Tolstoi, Sophocles and Chaucer."* The story about her school appeared in the *Sun-Times* on May 8, 1977, and it was picked up by other newspapers around the country. Later a visit by CBS-TV's *60 Minutes* drew tremendous viewer response. People were touched by the story of children who had been discarded as "unteachable" climbing to superior achievement in a school that was always short of books, paper, pencils, and even chalk.

In September 1981, Westside Preparatory School moved into its own permanent facilities along Chicago Avenue on the outskirts of Garfield Park. People saw it as a beacon of hope on the West Side, and they were proud of it.

Marva is sensitive to a child's needs and at the same time teaches the child subject matter and skills. That blend has always been the basis of her school.

CREATIVE ENCOUNTER #1 . . . . "Training" for Success

"Still it was a struggle to get her to read. She kept saying, 'I can't do it, I can't do it.' And I reminded her of the story 'The Little Engine That Could.' "

Think about a task, skill, or goal that you want to pursue. You may be a little afraid to tackle this new goal. In the sign write a goal that you want to accomplish. For example, I can give a good speech in front of my class.

In the first car write three strong reasons that make you think that you can successfully achieve your goal. In the caboose write three negative reasons that may limit your goal or cause you to doubt.

On another sheet of paper write about the impact of our choices of attitude. When our attitude is right, there's no valley too deep, no mountain too high.

"Train" yourself for success. Change your "train" of thought to the "I can" attitude. The "I can" attitude fuels the power for your potential to reach new peaks.

CREATIVE ENCOUNTER #2 . . . .**Attitude Choices**

Marva compiles lists of positive, motivating slogans to encourage her students. *"You are unique—there is no one else like you."*

Make up your own slogans about each of the following topics. Write them in calligraphy in the frames. Choose one of the slogans, and make your own decorative plaque as a special reminder.

1. *"Without the right attitude, everything else is wasted."* A significant decision we make on a day-to-day basis is our choice of attitude. We become what we think about. Write a slogan about attitude choices.

2. *"In the years since then I have been fighting an attitude, apathy."* Write a slogan that contrasts the concepts of a caring attitude with an apathetic attitude.

3. *"My big job with her was to awaken her enthusiasm."* Write a slogan about the contagious influence of an enthusiastic attitude.

CREATIVE ENCOUNTER #3 .... **Missteps to Success**

"You must never give up. Always try to fly."

Write one of your successes on top of the ladder. On the broken rungs write two failures or missteps you stumbled on before you reached that success. On the upper rungs write two small successes you achieved before you reached your ultimate goal.

Small successes are the building blocks to a fruitful life. You may miss your step and fall on those broken rungs but pick yourself up and climb to the next step.

Don't give up. Perseverance is success through trial and error. Climb the ladder to success, and discover new heights in your potential.

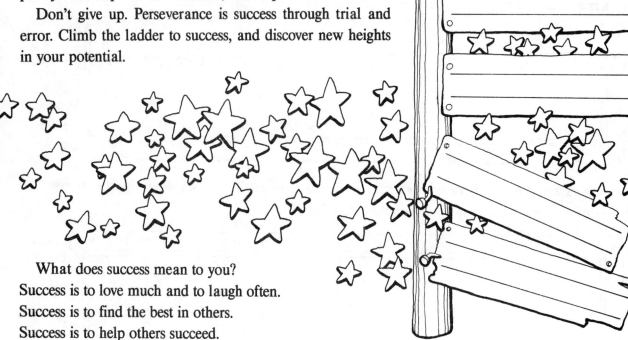

What does success mean to you?
Success is to love much and to laugh often.
Success is to find the best in others.
Success is to help others succeed.

Success is _____

Success is _____

Success is _____

Which is bigger, the fear of success or the fear of failure? _____

Why?_____

Which is the more difficult test, adversity or prosperity?_____

Why?_____

We slip and slide, falter and fail on those slippery stepping-stones. Nevertheless, keep on walking on that pathway to success. Stumbling blocks in your path are stepping-stones to the stars.

Flip your flops into success. On the back of this page, list at least three of your failures. Write at least one positive aspect about each failure and what you learned from each failure. Make a list of several of your successes.

CREATIVE ENCOUNTER #4 . . . . Teachable Moments

"You have to take stumbles before you can learn to walk. It's all right to make mistakes. I'm counting on you to help me with my mistakes, and I'll help you with yours."

How do you respond to your mistakes or failures? Are you self-critical and hard on yourself when you make mistakes? Or do you allow yourself to make mistakes and try to learn from them? Can you sometimes laugh at your mistakes? How teachable are you? What have you gained from those mistakes? Do you bounce back from your mistakes?

Strive to cultivate a teachable spirit. Make your mistakes into teachable moments. Ask yourself, what am I learning from this experience?

Marva was constantly reminding the children that some of the greatest people in history were ridiculed and told they would never amount to anything. For example, Louisa May Alcott, author of literary classics, was told by an editor that she would never write anything with popular appeal.

List several of these people and their obstacles. Write about these people in the form of prose, a poem, or a song to reflect the transition of failure to success.

CREATIVE ENCOUNTER #5 . . . . .A Commitment to Excellence

"We all shared in each other's success. The concept of self-determination goes hand in hand with self-discipline."

Marva believes the essence of teaching is to make learning contagious, to have one idea spark another. She sympathized with her students' fears and frustrations in school, told them she loved them, and then they had the choice of learning or sitting on the sidelines.

"Helping other people grow can become life's greatest joy," states Alan Loy McGinnis in *Bringing Out the Best in People.* The following are several of his rules for bringing out the best in people. Expect the best from people you lead. Make a thorough study of the other person's needs. Establish high standards for excellence. Create an environment where failure is not fatal. If they are going anywhere near where you want to go, climb on other people's bandwagons. Recognize and applaud achievement. Take steps to keep your own motivation high.

What happens when we're successful? Success brings more responsibility, stress, and criticism. Those are reasons people decide to avoid success and opt for mediocrity. Thomas Carlyle, the Scottish essayist and historian, declared for every hundred who can handle adversity, there's only one who can stand prosperity. Sudden elevation can bring difficulties: a false sense of pride and an inclination to walk over people, which can lead to a fall.

Are you willing to take a risk and walk on those stepping-stones to success in spite of the pitfalls? What are the dangers of equating our feelings of self-worth to our level of success measured by our performance? Are you willing to sacrifice to attain your goal?

You are the best you will ever be. Are you committed to being the best you? Are you committed to excellence in education? Do you find yourself avoiding personal achievement, like refusing to try out for the team, because you fear rejection? Is it better to try and fail or not to try and rest contently in past successes? Comment on the importance of the freedom to fail. How can you help others succeed?

Heed the advice of Bill Cosby in *You Are Somebody Special.* *"You can become successful, but first you must have some sort of feeling for it. How do you get a feeling for it? Sometimes the answer is 'try.' If you don't try, you will never know.*

"You CAN make it through if you keep moving forward and stay on the road. Your dreams CAN come true!

"The choices are up to you. The possibilities are wide open."

INDEPENDENT PROJECTS—COLLINS

1. Mary McLeod Bethune founded the small school that grew under her guidance into Bethune-Cookman College. Find similarities in Mary and Marva's experiences. Cite examples of how their students changed and progressed due to their influential gift of teaching.

2. *"My approach is to address a fault without ever attacking a child's character. Who they were was always separate and distinct from what they did. The gum chewing was displeasing, not the child."* List other rules and pedagogical methods and tools Marva implements in her classroom. Using what you have learned, become a teacher for a class period. Make arrangements to assist your teacher, tutor someone, or teach a small group of younger children. Prepare a lesson plan. Evaluate your learning experience as a teacher.

3. Marva sparked her students' interest in books, exposing them to a vast range of stories, topics, and authors. Step into the pages of an excellent book. Take the place of one of the characters in the story, and have someone ask you questions about what you think and feel as that character. Write a letter to one of the characters. Act out a fable or story. Expressively read aloud your favorite passages of a story.

4. Research the life of Benjamin Banneker, emphasizing his contribution to the planning of our nation's Capital. Design a brochure for Washington, D.C., with detailed illustrations of historical places of interest.

RESOURCE BOOKS—COLLINS

Collins, Marva, and Civia Tamarkin. *Marva Collins' Way.* Los Angeles: J.P. Tarcher, Inc., 1982.

Gillespie, Margaret C., and John W. Conner. *Creative Growth Through Literature for Children and Adolescents.* Columbus, Ohio: Charles E. Merrill Publishing Co., 1975.

Hartley, Fred. *Flops: Turn Your Wipeouts into Winners.* Old Tappan, New Jersey: Fleming H. Revell Co., 1985.

Holt, Rackham. *Mary McLeod Bethune.* Garden City, New York: Doubleday & Co., Inc., 1964.

Lewis, C.S. Edited by Lyle W. Dorsett and Marjorie Lamp Mead. *Letters to Children.* New York: Macmillan Publishing Co., 1985.

Lewis, Claude. *Benjamin Banneker: The Man Who Saved Washington.* New York: McGraw-Hill Book Co., 1970.

McGinnis, Alan Loy. *Bringing Out the Best in People: How to Enjoy Helping Others Excel.* Minneapolis: Augsburg Publishing House, 1985.

Shedd, Charles W., ed. 2nd ed. *You Are Somebody Special.* New York: McGraw-Hill Book Co., 1982.

Waitley, Denis. *The Double Win: Success Is a 2-Way Street.* Old Tappan, New Jersey: Fleming H. Revell Co., 1985.

_____ . *Seeds of Greatness: The Ten Best-Kept Secrets of Total Success.* Old Tappan, New Jersey: Fleming H. Revell Co., 1983.

Ziglar, Zig. *Steps to the Top.* Gretna, Louisiana: Pelican Publishing Co., Inc., 1985.

_____ . *Top Performance: How to Develop Excellence in Yourself and Others.* Old Tappan, New Jersey: Fleming H. Revell Co., 1986.

WALK FROM STRESS TO REST

STAN COTTRELL

"When I start getting low or when failure stares at me, I remember something that happened to me in 1982, near the end of my run across Europe. Despite my exhausted body that cried out for relief, I knew I could complete the run in the projected eighty days.

"Just then, I started up a steep mountain. As though the land had a personality, I screamed at it, 'You're not too high for me. I'm going to beat you because no mountain's too high!'

"I rethought my words. **No mountain too high.** *I picked up my pace. Those mountains almost won, but my hold-on attitude kept me going when I didn't think I could possibly take another step.*

"I've faced a lot of other mountains in life. And I still do. But I know none of them are too high. By sharing my experiences with you, my hope is that you'll also believe there's no mountain too high. It has become the theme of my life. I hope it will become yours."

BIOGRAPHICAL SKETCH

From early childhood Stan knew what it was to work from before sunrise till dark. His brother, four sisters, and Stan grew up on a farm near Munfordville, Kentucky. Their house was little more than a shack. Stan grew up believing that he disappointed his daddy in every way. A lot of punishment was meted out, because Stan simply wasn't growing the way his daddy thought he should. His father had been athletic and had excelled in basketball. He wanted a son to play basketball. His daddy usually humiliated Stan about his height after he had been drinking too much. When his father drank, his deep-seated anger boiled up, and he took out his hostility on his children.

Regardless of the early years, Stan loved and respected his father. Yet Stan never knew what it was to have his approval until late in his father's life. His father instilled in Stan the drive to succeed in spite of the odds. The really bright part of his growing up was his momma, who believed Stan was a special person and that he could achieve.

Winning the 100-yard dash at the age of twelve at a county fair changed the whole course of his life. At last Stan found something in which he could excel, and it was something he loved. When he was in the eleventh grade, Hart County sponsored a county-wide field meet, and he won several ribbons.

In 1978 Stan had run 405 miles across his home state of Georgia. Then came the 24-hour run in Atlanta in 1979, 167¼ miles, and the Run for America in 1980, 3,103.5 miles in 48 days from New York City to San Francisco. He had done several shorter runs in the South and across his native state of Kentucky. In 1982 he completed the Great European Friendship Run, 3,500 miles in 80 days from Edinburgh, Scotland, to the Rock of Gibraltar. Then followed more runs, two in the Dominican Republic and one in Jamaica. In 1984 Stan completed the Great Friendship Run from China's Great Wall north of Beijing to Guangzhous, 2,125 miles south in 53 days.

Lighthearted, outgoing, and good-humored, Stan is an internationally known ultramarathon runner who has logged over 130,000 miles throughout the world. Stan, his wife and three children reside in Tucker, Georgia. He is founder of Friendship Sports Association, a nonprofit organization which promotes the spirit of friendship and cooperation between peoples and nations through sports.

15

"While running across Europe this desire of mine came into sharp focus. It was as though the shutter of a camera opened for a split second, and I saw a sea of faces—people of varied backgrounds, all being friends with one another. That is when my biggest dream was born, Friendship Sports. I visualized whole nations being brought together as people from each country reach out to one another."

If you could visit any country, what country would you like to visit? Zip around the world in your imagination, and visualize yourself living in a foreign country. Share Stan's dream of lessening the stress and tension between the nations and building friendships. Stan will be touring your country the hard way in a friendship run. You will have some time to express your hospitality to him. He is very interested in your country.

Choose a foreign country. Using research and map skills, write about that country from the point of view as a citizen of that country. Complete these questions individually. Then share your information with your group.

1. What country do you live in?
2. What is a scenic spot that you would recommend Stan to see?
3. What kind of weather will Stan need to be prepared for?
4. What are some of your country's natural resources and exports?
5. What sports shine in your country?
6. Find some words in your language that you would like to teach to Stan.
7. Plan a meal to serve Stan. No monkey brain or snake, please.
8. Do you wear jogging shoes or wooden shoes? Describe your attire.
9. What is your school like?
10. Invite Stan to take a break from running and join you for a fun-filled time. Remember his feet are sore, so no jogging in wooden shoes. What do you do for recreation?
11. Describe a picturesque view of your home, inside and out.
12. What is one of your favorite family traditions that you will invite Stan to participate in?
13. Who are people from your country that have influenced the world?
14. Compare and contrast the heritage of America with that of your country.
15. If you could change anything about the government of your country, what would you change?
16. Imagine the President of the United States, the leader of your country, Stan, and you meeting together. What three steps would you like to take to constructively build communication and friendship among the people in the countries?

For further friendship running:

Role-play a conversation between Stan and you as a citizen of your foreign country.

Dramatize an adventuresome event on the friendship run.

Make a brochure of your country.

Plan a panel discussion. Divide into small groups. Each group will have citizens representing different countries. Your group can be composed of a representative of diplomats, homemakers, farmers, or people of other walks of life. Research and be prepared to discuss various issues from the point of view as a citizen from your chosen country. Dress as a citizen of that country. Hold the discussion for your classmates to hear. Discuss current events, freedom, war, government, economics, education, friendship sports, or other topics related to the above questions.

CREATIVE ENCOUNTER #2 ....Set Your Priorities

"At last I had gotten my priorities straight. I had a new outlook and my life started turning around."

What is important to you? What do you consider "top priority" in your life? All of us face the tyranny of urgent demands. It has a way of casting a shadow over the important. Quietly use this time for thinking and reflection. Thoughts disentangle themselves when spoken or put in ink. Written plans help to confirm right priorities. Keep this page available to you as a daily reminder.

Write down your priorities.

1. _____
_____
2. _____
_____
3. _____
_____
4. _____
_____
5. _____
_____

Write down the things you devote your time to, that is, how you spend your time.

1. _____
_____
2. _____
_____
3. _____
_____
4. _____
_____
5. _____
_____

Your above two lists will possibly conflict with each other. Therefore, think about some urgent demands in your life. Name a few to yourself. What important things are being ignored in your life because of the urgent? Write three ways you could change your schedule or your way of living to make room for these priorities. Be specific. Knowing and maintaining your priorities can help to reduce stress and give direction to your life.

1. _____
2. _____
3. _____

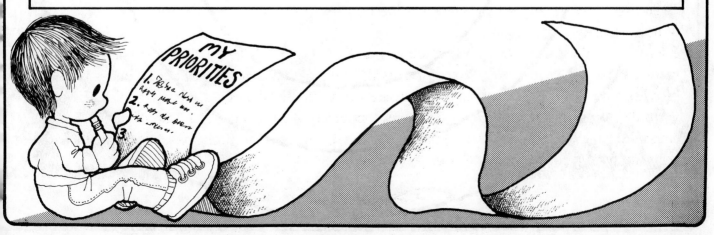

CREATIVE ENCOUNTER #3 .... Pace Yourself

"I had learned that the secret of endurance is to start slow. I have a theory I call Even Flow of Energy Distribution (EFED). Simply put, it means that I maintain a constant running level."

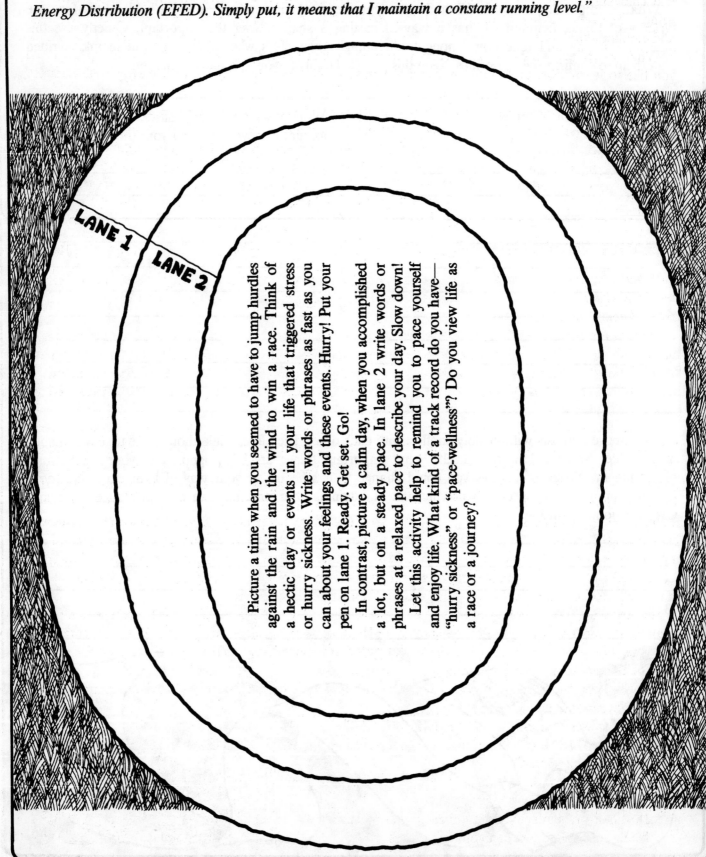

LANE 1

LANE 2

Picture a time when you seemed to have to jump hurdles against the rain and the wind to win a race. Think of a hectic day or events in your life that triggered stress or hurry sickness. Write words or phrases as fast as you can about your feelings and these events. Hurry! Put your pen on lane 1. Ready. Get set. Go!

In contrast, picture a calm day, when you accomplished a lot, but on a steady pace. In lane 2 write words or phrases at a relaxed pace to describe your day. Slow down!

Let this activity help to remind you to pace yourself and enjoy life. What kind of a track record do you have—"hurry sickness" or "pace-wellness"? Do you view life as a race or a journey?

CREATIVE ENCOUNTER #4 ....Speed Up

"As I got older, I realized how much running helped me cope with pain and stress. Even at seven years of age, running had become one of the most important things in my life."

Dr. Kenneth Cooper, director of the Aerobics Center in Dallas, encourages us to plan for a long and enjoyable life by living wisely and intensely each day through a balanced program of total well-being. *The Aerobics Program for Total Well-Being* focuses on the relationship between exercise, diet, and emotional balance.

What sports and kinds of exercise do you like to participate in and watch? What new sport would you like to learn? Research data on exercise, vitamins, food, and rest. On a chart plan a well-balanced exercise program designed especially for you.

Make a list of your favorite foods. Evaluate whether they are good sources of nutrition or not. On another chart plan several meals that would provide nutritional value.

Include specific, personal goals on your exercise and nutrition charts. Share your research and results and encourage your family, teachers, and friends to join you in maintaining a balanced exercise program. Set your pace and enjoy it. "Speed up" your exercise to "slow down" the stress factor in your life.

CREATIVE ENCOUNTER #5 ....Slow Down

"I had learned by then that running was my best therapy. Sometimes, when I didn't know how to handle a situation or when life became too hectic, I would go for a run, and when I came back, I always knew I could cope."

Stress is not always bad for us. Developing a good attitude can change a negative stressful situation into a positive one. We need to make the decision to choose not to be controlled by stressful circumstances. In other words, instead of stress controlling us, we need to do the best we can to manage stress. It seems we are never rid of some kind of stress, so it is necessary to learn to live with stress and to make good stress work for us. Let's strive to rest in stress.

In *Stress in Children* Dr. Bettie Youngs offers the following suggestions to help you cope with stress. Cultivate mental calmness. Draw vitality from stress. Make a conscientious effort to be an optimist. Turn problems into opportunities and obstacles into creative solutions. Focus awareness and total concentration on the task at hand. Be adventuresome. Try something you thought you could never do. Visualize yourself as vital and successful, a potential you. Relieve tension with action. Learn how to listen to the physical cues—warning signs that your body may be giving you. View constructive criticism as a means of self-improvement. Don't allow criticism to intimidate or offend you to the point of no action. Be aware of the importance of diet and nutrition. Cultivate an appreciation of self. Allow time for yourself. Slow down enough to allow others an opportunity to appreciate what is special about you. Take time to reenergize. Keep that quest and zest for life alive.

The following are other suggestions to help you cope with stress: Know yourself. Recognize your own limitations and live within those boundaries. Talk about your anxieties and frustrations with someone. Use your time wisely. Pace yourself. Get an adequate amount of sleep, and take a catnap for a renewed surge of energy. Keep a sense of humor.

Discuss these questions with your class. List the responses on the board to help you to understand stress, the wear and tear caused by life.

What causes stress?
When you are tired of waiting, a frantic schedule, or when a deadline for an unfinished project is drawing nearer?
What does stress do to you?
How can stress affect you physically?
How can stress affect your emotions or your behavior?
Name some ways you can cope with stress.

INDEPENDENT PROJECTS—COTTRELL

1. *"Running with the team and on my own became my major release from pressure. Floating along the roads, oblivious of everything else, I was free, really free."* What anxieties are in your pressure cooker? Draw a pressure cooker, and inside it list your anxieties. What ways work for you to release the pressure?

2. In what ways do you feel hurried? In *The Hurried Child*, David Elkind states that play is an antidote to hurrying. Write a fairy tale about a child who visited an imaginative, unhurried world of play and fantasy.

3. Research stress-related topics, such as the hurried child, Type A and Type B personalities, or the Holmes-Rahe test, the self-test for stress levels. Make your own gauge that monitors your stress level. Color the gauge to show your stress levels at various times.

4. Plan your own friendship run. Write a story map about your journey.

5. Create your own country. Use the questions in Creative Encounter #1 as a guideline to describe your imaginary country.

6. Conduct a debate concerning the following topics: a republic versus a dictatorship, capitalism versus communism, life in the land of freedom versus life behind the Iron Curtain, nuclear war versus land war.

7. Start your own recipe box of family favorites. Try to cook a meal for your family or friends. Give a demonstration to your class on how to make one of your favorite foods.

RESOURCE BOOKS—COTTRELL

Blitchington, W. Peter. *The Energy and Vitality Book.* Wheaton, Illinois: Tyndale House Publishers, Inc., 1981.

Cooper, Kenneth H. *The Aerobics Program for Total Well-Being.* New York: M. Evans and Co., Inc., 1982.

Cottrell, Stan. *No Mountain Too High.* Old Tappan, New Jersey: Fleming H. Revell Co., 1984.

_____ . *To Run and Not Be Weary.* Old Tappan, New Jersey: Fleming H. Revell Co., 1986.

Elkind, David. *The Hurried Child: Growing Up Too Fast Too Soon.* Reading, Massachusetts: Addison-Wesley Publishing Co., 1981.

Fixx, James F. *Jim Fixx's Second Book of Running.* New York: Random House, 1980.

Hanson, Peter G. *The Joy of Stress.* Kansas City, Missouri: Andrews, McMeel & Parker, 1986.

Hart, Archibald D. *Adrenalin & Stress: The Exciting New Breakthrough That Helps You Overcome Stress Damage.* Waco, Texas: Word Books, 1986.

Kimmel, Tim. *Little House on the Freeway: Help for the Hurried Home.* Portland, Oregon: Multnomah Press, 1987.

Lyttle, Richard B. *The Complete Beginner's Guide to Physical Fitness.* Garden City, New York: Doubleday & Co., Inc., 1978.

Sehnert, Keith W. *Stress/Unstress: How You Can Control Stress at Home and on the Job.* Minneapolis, Minnesota: Augsburg Publishing House, 1981.

Youngs, Bettie B. *Stress in Children: How to Recognize, Avoid and Overcome It.* New York: Arbor House, 1985.

WALK FROM POVERTY TO GENEROSITY

MARY CROWLEY

"When I founded Home Interiors, I made sure the company would be based on the idea of what it could give to others—to the women who sold the products, as well as the homes where those accessories went. As I went along, I used some of the profits to help others as well, in gratitude to God who had made our success possible. I dedicated the company to the purpose of helping others help themselves, enabling them to find joy as well as profit in their work. The result has been that even in the rough years, I've been rich in many ways.

"It was and is my theory that if you build the people, the people will build the business. If you help other people get what they want out of life, then you will get what you want out of life. I struggled to build this sense of 'otherness' into our sales force and urged all our employees to apply this nurturing attitude to their families as well."

Mary C. Crowley **BIOGRAPHICAL SKETCH**

Mary's mother died when she was eighteen months old, and she was sent to live with her loving grandparents on a Missouri farm. During those five years she received a fine heritage from them. When her father remarried, Mary and her older sister and brother moved to the state of Washington to live with them. She was deeply hurt by a stepmother who did not understand children and did not care to learn and a father who seemed oblivious to her needs. She counted as her greatest victory the fact that many years later when her father and stepmother were elderly, ill, and needed help, she was able to provide for them financially and care for them with forgiveness and love.

When she was thirteen, a juvenile court ordered that she be sent back to live with her grandparents, who were then farming in Arkansas. She did well at Fayetteville High School and graduated just after she turned seventeen. Desperately longing for a home and family of her own, Mary married immediately after graduating from high school, and soon she found herself alone with two small children, Don and Ruthie, to care for. With a $100 loan from the Rotary Club in Sherman, Texas, Mary made her way to Dallas. There she found work, education, warm friends and a loving new husband, Dave Crowley.

Hard work and open doors led her through accounting jobs to direct selling. With a $6,000 loan she launched her own company, Home Interiors and Gifts, on December 5, 1957. Her company grew into a business with more than 36,000 displayers and annual sales exceeding 500 million dollars. She was one of the most successful businesswomen in the country, one whose opinion was sought by everyone from President Reagan to her fellow board members at Mercantile National Bank. She received honors and accolades from the business, civic, and religious worlds.

There were times when Mary and her two children would have to eat cereal a week or two before payday. Nevertheless, she consistently gave a portion of her income to the church. Later she contributed millions of dollars to many whose special needs touched her heart. Her company helped their handicapped workers form their own company called Handi-Hands. As an extra Christmas present for the home office's 310 employees, $97,000 worth of groceries were given away.

Mary's exciting rages-to-riches success story did not come from a magic wand. It came from hard work, perseverance, a remarkable woman's indomitable spirit of victory and conquest, and her uncompromising commitment to excellence.

CREATIVE ENCOUNTER #1 . . . . .The Heart of the Home

"Love has a locale here on earth and it is called the home. Home is where love is nourished, where it is best expressed. Out of the home all other relationships are influenced.

"The home is the place where character is formed. In Home Interiors we feel the home should be a haven—a place of refuge, peace, harmony, and beauty. We encourage our people to develop attraction power in the home. Not only are we speaking of beautiful accessories and attractive colors but, more importantly, the attractiveness of the people who live there."

A house is built by hands, but a home is built by hearts. Home is truly where the heart is. Mary takes that one step further and says that the heart of that heart is the kitchen.

Create a recipe with essential ingredients to make a house a home. For example, 5 cups of commitment, 7 tablespoons of family time, and 3 pints of generosity. Write your recipe in calligraphy in the frame below. Decorate the space around your recipe with a special flair. Decorate your home with love. Frame your handiwork, and display it in your home to add a smile to your walls.

CREATIVE ENCOUNTER #2 ....Gifts from the Heart

"A giving, sharing attitude comes from the heart. When we have it, we are more aware of the other person's need than we are of what we may have to sacrifice. The first miracle of generosity takes place in the heart.

"We must be sure we do not wait until we have an abundance which to give and then make donations of the leftovers. An essential ingredient in sharing is sacrifice."

Don Carter, Mary's son, states, "A man is at his tallest when he stoops to help another." Mary suggests that we learn to give what is needed. Think of what the other person wants.

If there were no limitations in your potential to give, what material gifts would you like to give? What people, organizations, or charities would you help? What gifts from the heart would you like to give? Compassion, kindness, gentleness, and gratitude are gifts from the heart. What gifts would you give to the special people in your life? How would you like to help people with your money, talents, time, or service?

Draw illustrations on the presents to show what material gifts you would like to give to others. In the hearts draw illustrations to depict your gifts from the heart.

When we give of ourselves, we truly give. Carefully wrap your gifts from the heart with love, and give others these gifts to open and enjoy.

CREATIVE ENCOUNTER #3 . . . . .A Carefree Carousel

*"Worry is a misuse of the imagination. Don't live in 'if only' land. Instead of being an **if** thinker, become a **how** thinker."*

Worries seem to go around and around in your mind like a carousel. "If only . . ." "What if . . ." Spinning faster and faster, your feelings go up and down like the galloping horses to the music on a carousel.

Write down all your worries at random surrounding the carousel. After you are finished writing, imagine watching all our worries on that "Worry-A-Round." Slow down that worry whirlwind.

Since worry is a misuse of your imagination, refocus your imagination. Analyze each worry. If it is something you cannot change, try your best to accept it. If it is something you can change, think how you can get involved in that worry.

Change the "If only's" to "How to's." How can I deal with these worries? On the back of this page draw a "Carefree Freeway," and write your plan of action to relieve each worry.

Cast your worries to the wind. Watch that "Worry-A-Round" transform into a "Merry-Go-Round"— "A Carefree Carousel." Climb on a horse on that carousel and take off to new horizons on "Carefree Freeway."

CREATIVE ENCOUNTER #4 ....An Attitude of Gratitude

"Be grateful until you fairly glow. Gratitude is the heart's memory."

Mary suggests if you find that resentments and irritations are taking the place of gratitude and appreciation in your life, you might find it helpful to be thankful for the source of the irritation: your brother, sister, or bicycle. The possible rewards are greater happiness for you and for others as you find your own attitudes changing to those of gratitude and appreciation.

What are your resentments, frustrations, or worries? Think of the sources of these irritations. Make a list of these sources and other things for which you are thankful.

Add royalty to the routine. Little things make a person feel like "royalty." Write a thank-you note to someone special.

CREATIVE ENCOUNTER #5 ....Think Mink!

"When I first began Home Interiors I coined the phrase 'Think Mink.' Think the Best. Don't think rabbit, fox or squirrel. What I really meant was not to think materialistically but to remember that mink is the best. There is a natural abundance that is ours to have if we don't limit it by taking the 'little viewpoint.' Think big. Attempt great things. Believe big and you'll get big results.

*"The surest way to **find yourself** is to lose yourself in something **bigger than yourself!** Develop a sense of adventure.*

*"A lot of people believe it is better to set their goals low so that they won't fail. I say, set your goals high and fail if you have to. **Daring** generates **excitement, excitement** generates **enthusiasm,** and **enthusiasm** generates **energy.** People **like** to be around people with enthusiasm with a purpose."*

Make a list of your goals. Evaluate your goals. Applying Mary's principles, make another list with each of those goals set higher than your previous list.

Dare to think big. Generate your enthusiam and energy to take big steps to accomplish your goals.

CREATIVE ENCOUNTER #6 ....Dollars and Sense

"Money is a tool. What you do with it can bring a lot of joy.

*"If you work for the things you believe in, you are **rich,** though the way is rough. If you work only for money, you can never make quite enough.*

"Our labors should be rewarding, whether we are compensated for them or not. We must find joy in the work we do, whether we work at home or in a career. Then our work will not be a burden to us, and we will be free to really enjoy whatever other compensation it affords."

What are precious things in life that cannot be bought with silver or gold? Money can buy medicine, but not health. Money can buy a house, but not a home. Continue this list.

Talk about the distinction between your needs and wants. Define your number one weakness in handling your money. What is your most valued material possession?

What are your attitudes concerning money and work? Do you find joy in your work? Would you prefer a job with a large paycheck that you do not enjoy or a job which offers fulfillment with a considerably smaller paycheck?

Study the subject of money management. Keep a record of your spending to learn more about your spending habits. What ways can you earn money? Set up a budget. Decide how much money you want to give away, save, and spend.

Strive to learn to make sense with your dollars. Establish goals for your spending. Generosity and responsibility go hand in hand. Let generosity become your trademark. Be generous with your time, your efforts, your energy, your encouragement, and your money.

INDEPENDENT PROJECTS—CROWLEY

1. Coach Tom Landry of the Dallas Cowboys and Roger Staubach, former Dallas Cowboys quarterback, supported Mary in her multifaceted endeavors. They worked together with Don Carter, Mary's son who owns the Dallas Mavericks, to help build scholarship funds for young athletes. Read the biographies of Tom Landry and Roger Staubach. Work with a friend to make up a sports commentary about their lives to present to your class.

2. In *Decorate Your Home with Love*, Mary shows you how to exercise your creativity and individuality in decorating. Find out about these decorating tips. Research the topic of architecture. Design a blueprint and illustrate the exterior of your dream home. Draw detailed illustrations of the kitchen and the other rooms in a manner that reflects your interests, your taste, and your personality.

3. *"Color influences your life in endless, amazing ways, probably far more than you realize. The study of color is endlessly fascinating and deeply satisfying. Hold on for a happy ride around the color carousel."* Do a study of color. Find out how color affects your moods and how color makes a home come alive. Just as nature is divided into four seasons, you have a type of coloring that is most complemented by one of these seasonal palettes. Invite a color consultant to your class. Discover your season, and learn what colors make you look great.

4. *"I believe in America and the free enterprise system. I believe in the opportunities here in our country."* Lead a panel discussion on the effects of materialism in America, different views concerning allowances, financial planning, and other money issues.

RESOURCE BOOKS—CROWLEY

Ash, Mary Kay. *Mary Kay on People Management.* New York: Warner Books, Inc., 1984.

Burkett, Larry. *Your Finances in Changing Times.* Chicago: Moody Press, 1975.

Case, Richard T., Paul Meier, and Frank Minirth. *The Money Diet.* Richardson, Texas: Today Publishers, Inc., 1985.

Crowley, Mary C. *A Pocketful of Hope.* Old Tappan, New Jersey: Fleming H. Revell Co., 1981.

_____ . *Mary C. Crowley's Decorate Your Home with Love.* Old Tappan, New Jersey: Fleming H. Revell Co., 1986.

_____ . *String of Pearls: Secrets of Wisdom and Fulfillment.* Waco, Texas: Word Books, 1985.

_____ . *Women Who Win.* Old Tappan, New Jersey: Fleming H. Revell Co., 1979.

_____ . *You Can Too.* Old Tappan, New Jersey: Fleming H. Revell Co., 1980.

Jackson, Carole. *Color Me Beautiful.* (updated ed.) New York: Ballantine Books, 1984.

Ketterman, Grace H. *You Can Win over Worry.* Old Tappan, New Jersey: Fleming H. Revell Co., 1984.

St. John, Bob. *The Man Inside: Landry.* Waco, Texas: Word Books, 1979.

Staubach, Roger, and Frank Luksa. *Time Enough to Win: Roger Staubach.* Waco, Texas: Word Books, 1980.

WALK FROM LONELINESS TO CONTENTMENT

ROBIN GRAHAM

"As the lights of Honolulu faded, I spoke into the tape recorder. 'Leaving Mom and Dad this time was the hardest thing I've ever done. I wonder if I will ever see them again. I guess that saying good-bye to people you love always hurts. But it can't hurt more than I'm hurting now. I'm so homesick.'

"During the two years that I have sailed single-handed halfway around the world, I have weathered dismastings, hurricanes, a near collision with a freighter, and monotonous weeks slatting in the doldrums. But worst of all, I have tolerated the agony of loneliness. If only **Dove** *could talk, we'd make a perfect team.*

"Without Patti's encouragement I think I would have given up sailing. Each time I put out to sea along this dangerous coast, I wondered if I would ever see her again. I asked myself why I should go on taking such risks. But Patti gently reminded me of my commitment. Later, I was to see how amazingly God cared for me."

BIOGRAPHICAL SKETCH

On Robin's tenth birthday his dream came true, for he sailed a boat for the very first time. His parents had given him a white-hulled dinghy with a mast and a single red sail. After school each day when other kids went off to play baseball and soccer, he would run down and take out his dinghy. Within a week he was sailing by himself. He began to master all sorts of sailing skills. He couldn't soak up enough knowledge about sailing.

Three years later his parents, Robin, and his brother spent thirteen months cruising the South Pacific on the *Golden Hind*. They returned to California with suntans, lots of stories, and an even deeper passion for the sea, for sailing, and for exploring. Robin and his dad then sailed from California to Hawaii. In those days his dad was his hero figure. He taught Robin seamanship and navigation.

One of Robin's class projects was to read the *Adventures of Huckleberry Finn*. Robin and two friends decided to have their own Huckleberry Finn adventure. They fixed up an old sixteen-foot aluminum lifeboat, sailed without telling their parents, and ignored a storm warning. The Coast Guard desperately searched for the three teenaged boys feared lost at sea. His parents were concerned that Robin might be tempted to venture to sea in an unsafe boat again, so they invested in a 24-foot sloop called *Dove*.

Robin's dream was to sail around the world alone. On July 27, 1965, Robin, at the age of sixteen, set sail from San Pedro, California, in *Dove* with his two kittens named Joliette and Suzette. Robin was grateful that his parents trusted him and gave him this opportunity for adventure. Less than 24 hours after he set sail for Hawaii, Robin had second thoughts, but he never gave up. Many people had been good to Robin in faraway places. He met many people living on the different islands and in Africa, who enjoyed life so much, even though they had so little. His journey around the world had taken 1,749 days, and he traveled 30,600 miles.

Robin is now a carpenter. He lives in the Montana wilderness with his wife Patti, whom he met during his voyage, and a daughter Quimby and a son Benjamin. Robin built a log cabin for his family with his own hands. They found pioneer-style living rough, but through perseverance and Patti's encouragement and cheer, the test of endurance was won. Robin found a new way of life by which he can support his family and live in harmony with the land.

CREATIVE ENCOUNTER #1 ....A Treasure Map

"The greatest adventure of my life began with a daydream. Several weeks before my tenth birthday I was sick in bed with the flu and was feeling pretty miserable. I lay back on the pillows and looked at a picture on the opposite wall—a picture of a small boat with a red sail.

"Of course, I knew the boat in the picture had not actually moved, but my heart thumped with excitement while I played the game of make-believe. I imagined that I was the navigator of the boat. I closed my eyes and saw myself sailing to a faraway island with golden beaches. I pictured diving off the anchored boat into a blue lagoon and pretended that I found the wreck of an old pirate ship. Jewels and gold coins filled the treasure chest I discovered."

Imagine that you are on this faraway island that Robin described. On the back of this page draw a map of this island. Locate on a globe where you would like this island to be. Name your island. On this island draw a maze of paths and obstacles to overcome that lead to a treasure chest. Draw a waterfall, animals, fish, cliffs, caves, a shipwreck, beaches, forests, lagoons, and mountain ranges on your island.

On a separate sheet of paper make up various clues that go along with your treasure map. Create your clues with a flavor of risk, danger, and adventure. Give these clues to a friend for him to follow to the treasure chest. In the space below draw a treasure chest and unique things you would like to find in it.

Close your eyes. As your teacher reads the imaginative journey, visualize yourself with Robin sailing around the world.

Pantomime scenes from your imaginative journey around the world. Draw illustrations of some of nature's jewels.

Imaginative Journey Around the World

At the moment when the kittens and you are feeling most miserable in the heat of windless days, you are surprised by visitors. The kittens immediately prick up their ears to listen to an unusual, high-pitched squeak. Perhaps they think that they hear Supermouse! But no, it isn't Supermouse. Your visitors are porpoises. You stand for the longest time, shouting and laughing at their antics, and forgetting how bad you had felt only minutes before. One porpoise stands up on its tail and smacks its fins as if it is clapping for you. You clap too. After the porpoises have splashed about the boat for a quarter of an hour, they suddenly dash away.

At the Tonga Islands the sea is so clear and the sand so white that it proves the perfect place for snorkling. You discover a whole new world under the surface of the water. Shoals of brilliantly colored fish dash past you, and the coral formations look like magical gardens created by Walt Disney. It is here that you start your shell collection. Because you are always on the lookout for different varieties, each dive is a treasure hunt. Soon you have five shoe boxes of nature's jewels.

Now *Dove* sits in the water like a toy boat in a bathtub. A spell of absolute calm—just no wind at all—is almost as frustrating as the contrary winds. Suddenly you freeze with fear. About three miles off the port side, a huge, black, snakelike thing is climbing out of the sea. An undulating column reaches out of the water to a height of about 2000 feet and then spreads into a black line of jagged clouds. No, it is not a sea monster. It is a twister. This waterspout, as sailors call it, is the first cousin of a tornado. The deadly twister, the most feared peril of the high seas, is coming toward you! There seems to be no way to escape. Your heart pounds as you realize that the gap between *Dove* and the evil-looking monster is shrinking. *Dove* heels right over as the wind force increases. But then suddenly *Dove* swings back onto an even keel. The wind dies. The twister unexpectedly changes direction. It now moves away from you.

As you sail for Africa, you glance at the horizon over the stern and see a ridge of black clouds approaching rapidly. Within an hour the azure blue sky is blacked out all over and the sea suddenly begins to get very rough. The sea behaves like a boxer between rounds—panting, resting, and gathering strength for the next attack. The surface swirls and then lashes out again with waves cresting thirty or more feet above the trough. Hissing whitecaps pour green water across the deck. In the fading light of the second day of the storm, the huge swells seem to be like enormous wild animals, brutal and waiting for their chance to destroy a small boat that dares to be out of this water. Peals of thunder roar like the sound of an express train rolling over a metal bridge. Brilliant flashes of lightning illuminate monster waves and fill the cabin with an eerie green light. After collapsing from fatigue onto the bunk, you drift off into a deep sleep. You are awakened by sunlight pouring through the portholes. Miraculously the wind had dropped fifteen knots. The sea is gentle, sparkling, and beautiful.

As soon as you arrive on the Galápagos Islands, you begin to explore these exciting islands, where most of the animals have no fear of human beings because they are protected. The sea lions play games just like kids on a playground. Although they aren't really tame, one sea lion picks up a stick and has a great underwater tug of war with you—a tussle that he eventually wins. You are fascinated with watching the sea lions, for they are terrific surfers. The mockingbirds are so tame they fly to your shoulders. It is all so beautiful that it is like a dream world.

At night the sea is lit by the phosphoresence of tiny living creatures. Watching these little flashlights streaming out in the wake of *Dove* reminds you of traveling over a city in an airplane. Stars twinkle as brightly as diamonds. Because the air at sea is so much cleaner than it is over land, the luminous dots appear much brighter and nearer than usual. In fact, you feel you could almost reach up and pluck them out of the black velvet of the night sky, even though many of them are millions of light years away.

There were memorable nights at sea, many of them beautiful beyond imagination. Then there were the days—far, far more than you could have hoped for—when *Dove* scudded along over azure-blue waters, days when the spirit of freedom seemed to touch you with her wings.

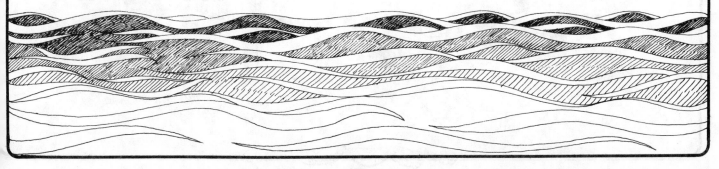

CREATIVE ENCOUNTER #3 ....Survival and Sandcastles

The top editor of *National Geographic* encouraged Robin to continue his voyage at a time when Robin was considering the possibility of quitting. *"So many people are vicariously sailing with you, people who've never even sailed a boat across a lake. So many teenagers like you have been saying that there are no new frontiers to cross and no new Everests to climb. But you've shown them that there are still adventures for the adventurous. If you gave up now, you'd be letting yourself down and disappointing a lot of people who believe in you."*

1. Name some situations in your own life when you had the support of others, but yet you "sailed" alone (first day of school, your first speech). _____

    _____

2. What new frontiers would you like to cross (learn a new skill, take a trip around the world)? _____

    _____

3. Robin was committed to the challenge of sailing around the world, even though it was a struggle to survive at times. Would you prefer a challenge or career that offers ease and comfort, but it is not very enjoyable for you? Or would you prefer a challenge or career where you might have to sacrifice some of your needs and comforts, but it is fulfilling and enjoyable for you? _____

    Elaborate on your response. _____

    _____

    _____

    _____

4. Robin experienced the haunting feeling of survival at sea and financial hardship in looking for a means of living off the land in Montana. What are other ways that people experience the survival stage of life (loneliness, hunger, illness)? _____

    _____

5. You have worked hard to survive and built a sandcastle (your dream). Then the secure structure is toppled over due to a gigantic wave. You are suddenly alone back in the survival stage again. The reasons for the destruction of your dream could be financial setbacks or loss of securities.
    Imagine rebuilding a sandcastle on golden beaches. On the back of this page draw a sturdy sandcastle to represent your dream. Write your thoughts in a sentence or two in the path leading to your sandcastle about trying to survive and building the sandcastle of your dreams.

" 'I can't be seasick,' I thought. 'I'm never seasick, or hardly ever.' Then I realized what my problem was. It was homesickness. I was feeling an aching loneliness. Often throughout my voyage I was to experience the same symptoms. Loneliness was to grip me for a thousand days and nights. At times it was almost as if loneliness climbed aboard **Dove** with cold, clammy hands that reached out for my throat and heart and stomach. Loneliness was to be an enemy that I never quite managed to conquer. The enemy knew my weakest moments. It knew exactly when to strike."

Just as Robin and *Dove* were tossed and turned by the wind and waves, adversities will push their way into your life. You will need to learn to flow with those adversities.

Swiss psychiatrist Paul Tournier called loneliness *"the most devastating malady of this age."* In *How to Win Over Loneliness* John Haggai states that loneliness is complex. It is different from being alone. One can be alone by choice, but even when it is not by choice, being alone can be creative and productive. But being lonely is usually not by choice; it can drain the emotions and negate creativity. He believes that loneliness will find it difficult to survive in the mind that is goal-oriented, the heart that is service-oriented, and the will that is highly motivated. Kill loneliness through friendliness. Be determined to be a friend. Be real in your relationships. Make the art of friendliness and friend-making a lifelong pursuit.

In *Loneliness Is Not a Disease*, Tim Timmons states that the decision to uncover loneliness with all of its masquerades (despression, anxiety, guilt, anger, etc.) is the decision to love! When you decide to relieve your loneliness, you must also decide to release your love. You will periodically visit the state of loneliness in life, but you do not have to live there. Since loneliness is a decision and not a disease, there is hope!

Robin counteracted his loneliness with keeping busy, reading, cooking, sleeping, or listening to the radio and the sounds of the sea. The schools of porpoises that visited him seemed to understand a schoolboy's homesickness, smiled up at him and squeaked encouragement as they gamboled around the craft.

The authors of *Why Be Lonely* offer practical advice to overcome loneliness. Make life a growing process. Live one day at a time. Have an understanding for other people. Accept imperfections in others. Learn to be forgiving. Share your problems with someone. Never give up on yourself. Become aware of your loneliness. Practice mature communication of your feelings with others.

Use the above information and the following questions for a class discussion. What color is loneliness? What are lonely sounds? If you could touch loneliness, what would it feel like? What type of weather would describe the chill of loneliness? How does it feel to be "shipwrecked" by loneliness?

What is the difference of being alone and loneliness? When does loneliness occur in your own life? What do you do when it occurs? Do you think a change of scenery, a change of job or position, or the purchase of new possessions will help to relieve the pain of loneliness temporarily or permanently? Why? How does self-centeredness relate to loneliness? Do you think people can be lonely in crowds. Why or why not? When have you been struck by homesickness?

What are causes of loneliness? What advice would you give to overcome the devastating pain of loneliness? Talk about the loneliness of being misunderstood, carrying your burden alone, standing alone for right, or other kinds of loneliness.

INDEPENDENT PROJECTS—GRAHAM

1. *"With me, as it surely was with Columbus, a flame of longing to travel and explore faraway lands blazed in my mind and heart."* If you could sail around the world, where would you sail? Gather resource books about the places you would like to visit. Make a diorama to portray a scene from your voyage of explorations.

2. What would you want to include in your survival kit for an exploration on land, sea, or in space? List various supplies, books, tools, navigation instruments, food, etc., you would include for your exploration. Prioritize your list in the order of what is most important, and state reasons why you placed them in that particular order.

3. What type of adventurer would you like to be—an explorer, a sailor, or an astronaut? Research the stories of Christopher Columbus or other adventurers. Use the information about them to write an imaginative adventure story of your "own" explorations.

4. Would you prefer to live in a pioneer style of living like Robin and Patti's family or in a city? Contrast the life-style of living in the country to a city. State the advantages and disadvantages of each life-style.

5. Ask other people about lonely times in their lives and the causes of their loneliness. Express your thoughts in a poem or some form of creative writing about new insights you have gained about loneliness from these people. Reach out and find someone who is especially lonely now, and share what you have learned to help them.

RESOURCE BOOKS—GRAHAM

Carter, W. Leslie, Paul D. Meier, and Frank B. Minirth. *Why Be Lonely? A Guide to Meaningful Relationships*. Grand Rapids, Michigan: Baker Book House, 1982.

Constable, George, ed. *Cruising*. New York: Time-Life Books, 1975.

Graham, Robin Lee. "A Teen-ager Sails the World Alone." *National Geographic*. October 1968, pp. 445-491.

_____ . "Robin Sails Home." *National Geographic*. October 1970, pp. 504-545.

_____ . "World-roaming Teen-ager Sails On." *National Geographic*. April 1969, pp. 449-493.

Graham, Robin, and Derek Gill. *The Boy Who Sailed 'Round the World Alone*. Waco, Texas: Word Books, 1985.

Graham, Robin Lee, and Derek Gill. *Dove*. New York: Harper & Row, 1972.

_____ . *Home Is the Sailor*. New York: Harper & Row, 1983.

Haggai, John. *How to Win Over Loneliness*. Minneapolis: Jeremy Books, 1979.

Halliburton, Richard. *Richard Halliburton's Complete Book of Marvels*. Indianapolis, Indiana: The Bobbs-Merrill Co., Inc., 1960.

George, M.B. *Basic Sailing*. New York: Hearst Marine Books, 1984.

Timmons, Tim. *Loneliness Is Not a Disease*. New York: Ballantine Books, 1981.

WALK FROM DISCOURAGEMENT TO DETERMINATION

SALLY HADDOCK

"The decision to become a vet didn't really come out of left field. In fact, it was more discovery than decision, and I suppose that's true of the best career choices. When all my other career notions were chipped away, what remained was an aspiring vet. I had dreamed about becoming a vet ever since childhood, but had always assumed it would be impossible for me to be accepted by a veterinary college.

"It is not easy to become a veterinarian. But once I'd settled on it, I wanted to become one more than anything in the world. I truly loved animals, but it was more than that. I loved the intricacies of science. I liked knowing how a stray amoeba could wreak havoc with a digestive system. I liked understanding the delicate mechanism of life. Veterinary medicine offered the answers I missed in psychology. It was more practical than zoology. It was a 'hands-on' science with a clear goal."

Sally Haddock

BIOGRAPHICAL SKETCH

Sally was determined to become a veterinarian. In order to meet the unofficial requirements for admittance to a vet school, she desperately needed a job with a veterinarian. She had no connections in the field. She also didn't have a 4.0 average, which some of the rejecting vets whom she approached for a job found shocking. One out of every ten applicants would be accepted to vet school. Friends, teachers, veterinarians, and even passersby had told her that it was just too difficult, too competitive, and too demanding.

Sally learned determination counts. After graduation from Miami University in Oxford, Ohio, she was accepted at the Ohio State University College of Veterinary Medicine in Columbus. She was up against stiff competition, and in fact competition became a constant undercurrent in the four years of training. While in veterinary college, Sally's pets, Watson the rabbit and a ten-foot boa constrictor named Stephanurus Dentatus, often caused friction among her roommates.

Sally's life as a veterinarian entails stories from her heroic attempt to save dying Bunny Celeste, whose heartbroken owner had given her up for lost, to saving the life of a high-rise cat, Puffy, who survived a precipitous plunge and was found to have swallowed a nickel as well, to the challenge of concealing a boisterous Great Dane, convalescing in the back of a Ukrainian restaurant until a family could be found for him. She also de-quilled porcupine victims, treated cows for hardware disease, and did a necropsy on a cat that had swallowed a cassette tape. One Christmas she helped to reunite a beloved dog, Sanford, with his owners who had to give him up because they couldn't afford the operation he needed.

Sally's determination, love, patience, and devotion for animals enabled her to overcome people's discouraging remarks to give up her dream, the rigors of veterinary college, and the trials of hands-on training, which brought her to the famed New York Animal Medical Center. Sally, her husband, Tom Birchard, and daughter, Kristen Emily, reside in Manhattan. She is owner and veterinarian at St. Marks Veterinary Hospital in the East Village.

Pet loss is the most difficult part of Sally's profession. Her heart-warming story is filled with the joys and heartaches of being a veterinarian and the personal triumphs of fulfilling her lifelong dream.

CREATIVE ENCOUNTER #1 ....Pet Pals

"After all, pets are in most cases beloved friends."

Isn't it fun to have "real" and "unreal" animals as companions? A teddy bear or your favorite stuffed animal that may have a missing nose or torn paw due to many hugs provides years of security and comfort in the growing-up years.

Create your own pet pals. Combine a stuffed animal or an animal figurine with other objects. Name your pet pals. Here are examples. Combine a stuffed animal with an alarm clock. How will your "Alarminal" wake you up in the morning? Create a pet car in the shape of a mustang or a cougar. A rocking horse on a merry-go-round, "A Rock-Around," could make you dizzy. Combine stuffed animals with slippers, and your "slippets" will keep you warm. Design your very own pet rocks or pet shells. The kitchen can be filled with pet pals: a cookie jar in the shape of cat, a honey jar in the shape of a bear, or an oven mitt shaped like a fish. How about a music box inside a teapot shaped like a duck that pours through the bill? Relax and enjoy tea for two with your "musical quackpot."

Try to develop flexibility in your thinking. Draw your own pet pal in the space below. Make up an advertisement about your pet pal, and present it to your class.

CREATIVE ENCOUNTER #2 . . . . The Talking Animal Kingdom

"I found myself, as I so often do, wishing that Bunny Celeste could speak up. I wanted Walt Disney."

Have you often wished you could talk to animals? Would you like to know what animals think and how they feel? Now is your opportunity for your fantasy to become real. Enter the animal kingdom in your imagination, where you can talk to the animals. Notice their expressions and gestures. Listen to the mischievous monkey chattering. A fawn is curiously staring at you with a playful twinkle in her eyes. An eagle soars above you expressing his free spirit. A dolphin is ready to offer you a ride to the underwater world. A peacock proudly stalks in a king-like manner with an array of brightly colored feathers shaped like a giant fan.

What would you like to talk about with these animals? Draw various animals. By each animal write in a few words that you think the animal would say. Extend this activity by planning a puppet show. Divide into small groups. Write a script for a puppet show or try your hand at an impromptu performance with a conversation between a human and animals. Decide who wants to be the human voice talking to the animals and who wants to play the parts of the animals. Perform your puppet show for your class with animal puppets and stuffed animals. Name your animals. Vary the range of your voices and dialects. Priscilla, the poodle, might greet you with a deep voice and sophisticated accent, *"How do you do?"* Pudgy Porker, the piglet, might greet you with a high voice and twang, *"Howdy!"*

CREATIVE ENCOUNTER #3 . . . . Pet Pen Pals

"When the moose arrived it shattered all my moose stereotypes. It was shaggy and shy and looked a lot like Bullwinkle. As it was a young moose, it hadn't yet reached the skyscraper proportions of the adult, which can tower over six feet at the shoulder and weigh as much as a Volkswagen. And it immediately endeared itself to me because it was an easy diagnosis. It was obvious at first glance what was wrong: he had a broken leg. Perhaps it was the pain, perhaps fear, but this moose was as cool and composed as his wall-mounted brethren."

Bring animal cheer to another. With your pen in hand, draw a pet to send to a pal. Make a special card for someone using some kind of humorous association with an animal. Write your animal greeting cards in calligraphy. Here are examples. Draw the moose that Sally helped. Write inside the card, I "moose" you very much. Please get well and come back soon. Draw a bear hanging from a tree with two paws. Write inside the card, I am "bearly" making it without you. Draw a bear with her paw inside a trunk of a tree searching for honey. Her cubs are innocently looking up at their mother with bees swarming near her. The mother devotedly sacrifices the risk of the bee stings to give honey to her cubs. In a heart write, Love "bears" all things!

Stop "monkeying" around. Try your "paw" (hand) at animal greeting cards. "Bear" in mind "ewe" especially need your creative energy for this activity. Let's "fish" for new ideas.

P.S. Don't let them "buffalo" "ewe." You "otter" enjoy this!

Animals can enrich our lives and teach us much about our own nature. Liven up your day with a fun combination of a couple of our favorite things in life: creativity and animals. Choose a few of these activities that you would like to do. Let your imagination soar like an eagle.

If you could choose an animal to help Sally in her veterinary practice, what animal would you choose? Why? How about a baboon, because intelligence and cleanliness are among his most favorable attributes.

What kinds of animals are you like? Why? Make a list of your characteristics that can be compared to animals. Here are examples: loyal like a dog or bad-tempered like a rhinoceros. After you have your list of animals, draw a combination of all of them in an illustration of one unique animal.

Are you a lark or a night owl? Do you function best in the morning hours or evening hours? What are the advantages and disadvantages of being a morning or night person?

Match pets with people. Make a list of careers. What pets go along with their careers? Here are examples: a policeman, a German Shepherd; a musician, a canary; a parachutist, a pelican; a race car driver, a cheetah; an acrobat, an orangutan.

If you could teach a giraffe to dribble a basketball, what do you think would happen? How would the cheetah do in a competitive race in the Olympics? What other animals would be good at sports? Make up rules for your animal sporting event. Make a diorama of your animal in action at this event.

If you could teach an octopus to do your chores, how fast do you think he could finish them? Just think, he could do eight chores at the same time. Draw an octopus doing your chores.

There she is—Miss Sophie, the sophisticated chinchilla dressed in her latest luxurious fur at a glamorous fashion show in Mink's Fashion Mart. Greet Mr. Debonair, a suave penguin in his spiffy tuxedo, and Mrs. Ella, the elegant alligator dressed with her own stylish accessories—an alligator belt, purse, and boots. Design fashionable clothes for the show with a variety of animals. Name your animals and designer clothes. Label the prices on the clothes, and write a description about the models and their wardrobe to present to your class. Have a beauty contest between your models.

Jump inside the pouch of Mama Kangaroo and see the world through the eyes of her baby. Write about your bounding and pounding experience. Which is more fun, being in midair or landing?

The Masked Bandit strikes again. The suspect is a sneaky raccoon that has been stealing cookies and dunking sweets in milk. This cuddly creature washes his food and any trace of paw prints, which makes him difficult to be tracked. Organize an agency of animal spies to investigate the mystery of the Masked Bandit.

A woodpecker should not open a door in a tree house without knocking first. A squirrel chatters with her neighbor, but she should be careful not to chat about the latest gossip in the animal kingdom. An elephant gentleman should use his trunk to open Jeep doors for the passengers to go on a safari. A parrot should remember to say please and thank you, when she asks for a cracker. Make a list of other animal manners for the Animal Charm School.

Otters are nature's fun-loving clowns. They will take turns sliding down a wet hill. A few minutes later, otters will be playing Follow the Leader or starting a wrestling match with their brothers and sisters. Otters take time to train their young. The otter can take life seriously but also enjoys life. We should not forget to laugh, play, and enjoy ourselves. Draw otters clowning around. Write a motto about enjoying life.

Enter the Animal Hall of Fame. Make a list of famous animals in the movies, on television programs, and in cartoons. Create your own animal cartoon character.

"When I think about putting pets to sleep—unquestionably the most difficult part of my job—I think about Sunshine, the yellow Lab. Rarely have I seen a more touching parting, as the little boy threw his arms around Sunshine's neck and the girl, crying, kissed her big wet nose.

"Any vet would have difficulty with the situation, but for me it was even worse because usually, when I have to watch people go through this sort of thing, I begin to cry as well. No matter how many times I've been through it, it never fails to touch me."

What does a pet mean to you? A pet is a companion who accepts you and is nonjudgmental. A pet will cuddle up and reassure you that you are loved, even if you make a poor grade or have the chicken pox. A devoted pet teaches you about love, loyalty, birth, life, and death. Training and caring for a pet makes you feel important as you learn to carry responsibility. Your valuable friend gives you a feeling of belonging and a sense of pride. Furthermore, a sense of security is derived from the protection that many pets provide.

The authors of *Pet Loss* state that crying and feeling lonely or depressed are natural ways of responding to the death of a pet that has shared your daily life. The response to death involves disbelief and denial at first and then crying, bewilderment, anger, guilt, depression, and attempts to rationalize the loss. Some other symptoms of grief are fear of abandonment, nightmares, insomnia, and anger toward siblings and playmates. Learning problems in school can also develop, stemming from lack of concentration brought on by anxiety.

You may be reassured that grief and mourning are normal. Knowing that animals have shorter life spans than humans, that they live more perilous lives and that some illnesses cannot be controlled will help the owner accept the loss and put it into perspective. The authors of *Pet Loss* suggest that you try to openly show and share your feelings, no matter how silly they seem. It may comfort you to try to keep the pet's memory alive. Look through photograph albums for pictures of your pet. What special requests do you have for funeral services or burial? Some people are not ready to substitute a new animal for a loved pet, while others find it important to do so quickly.

If you choose to talk at school about the loss of your pet, hold a group discussion about the incident. This will allow your friends to share similar experiences and provide reassurance that you are not alone.

It is not only difficult to lose your own pet, but also to see animals that are in trouble or that are suffering. Unexpected feelings of sadness and compassion can sweep upon you when you encounter a baby robin pounced upon by a hungry cat; the lonely eyes of an orphan animal seeking refuge; the once majestic stature of a deer now lying helplessly on the side of a road; a once carefree, wild animal now locked in a cage; a frisky dog with a terminal illness; a crying kitten taken away from her mother; or a timid, fearful pet that has been neglected or abused. When you come upon a wild baby animal in trouble, have you wondered what to do? When have you encountered an animal that needed special care or help? In what ways could the animal have been helped?

Express your thoughts and feeling about your pet and/or pet loss in writing and drawings. Write about the days when your pet first came into your family, reminisce about shows or ribbons, how hard it was to train the pet, and funny things that happened with your pet. Write an epitaph for your pet. Draw a shape that is associated with your pet. Inside the shape draw an illustration of a memorable moment with your pet. For example, inside the shape of a bone draw your puppy, when he was playfully making friends with a kitten.

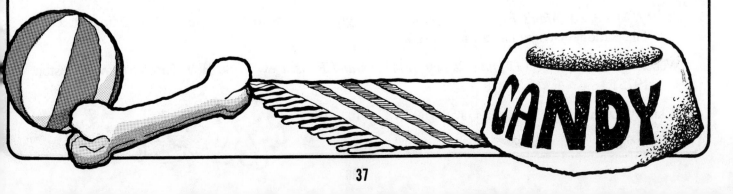

INDEPENDENT PROJECTS—HADDOCK

1. *"If you lavish attention on it while it's a pup, talk to it, introduce it to lots of people, show it affection, train it and give it tasks to do, you'll be rewarded with a companion that will never disappoint you."* If you could own and take care of a pet, what pet would you choose? Would you like fur, fins, or feathers? Make a file of factual information about the care and training of your pet.

2. Research the safety of animals, wild orphan babies, and the world's endangered wildlife. On a poster draw a large building, an orphanage for animals. Draw a different animal looking out each window. Beside each forlorn animal write what each one would like to say to human beings.

3. Make up a gameboard decorated with circus animals, farm animals, zoo animals, and animals in the mountains, forests, and oceans. On cards ask questions about animals, such as, What is a joey? What does porcine mean? Use a spinner. Take turns. The first one who makes it to the end wins.

4. *"Our freshman year had been devoted to basic courses in anatomy, physiology, chemistry, pharmacology, pathology, embryology and the like."* What are the meanings of these subjects? Read about the cases that a veterinarian encounters. How does a person become a veterinarian? Find out how to write a resumé. Write a fictitious veterinarian's resumé to show the steps that it takes to become a veterinarian.

5. Plan a program for Pet Day. Display your work about pets. If possible, bring your pets and stuffed animals to school. Tell about your pets. Invite a veterinarian to talk about his/her career. Sing songs that talk about animals. Watch a movie, such as *Old Yeller.*

RESOURCE BOOKS—HADDOCK

Chrystie, Frances N. *Pets: A Complete Handbook on the Care, Understanding, and Appreciation of All Kinds of Animal Pets.* 3d rev. ed. Boston: Little, Brown and Co., 1974.

Curtis, Patricia. *Animal Doctors: What It's Like to Be a Veterinarian and How to Become One.* New York: Delacorte Press, 1977.

Embery, Joan, and Denise Demong. *My Wild World.* New York: Delacorte Press, 1980.

Haddock, Sally, and Kathy Matthews. *The Making of a Woman Vet.* New York: Simon and Schuster, 1985.

Herriot, James. *The Best of James Herriot: The Favorite Stories of One of the Most Beloved Writers of Our Time.* New York: St. Martin's Press, 1982.

Laycock, George. *The World's Endangered Wildlife.* New York: Grosset & Dunlap, Inc., 1973.

Messmann, Jon. *Choosing a Pet.* New York: Grosset & Dunlap, Inc., 1973.

Nieburg, Herbert A., and Arlene Fischer. *Pet Loss: A Thoughtful Guide for Adults and Children.* New York: Harper & Row, 1982.

Quackenbush, Jamie, and Denise Graveline. *When Your Pet Dies: How to Cope with Your Feelings.* New York: Simon and Schuster, 1985.

Severy, Merle, ed. *Man's Best Friend: National Geographic Book of Dogs.* rev. ed. Washington, D.C.: The National Geographic Society, 1966.

Weber, William, J. *Wild Orphan Babies: Mammals and Birds.* New York: Holt, Rinehart and Winston, 1975.

Whitney, Leon. *Pets.* New York: David McKay Co., Inc., 1971.

WALK FROM DEPRESSION TO JOY

TIM HANSEL

"What a test of character adversity is. It can either destroy or build up, depending on our chosen response. Pain can either make us better or bitter.

"I had a choice. I knew by now that the damage was permanent, and that pain would be a companion for the rest of my journey. The life I'd always known was never to be again.

"Slowly my rage to live emerged from the depression, frustration, and anger. But when it was there I realized that it had a taste to it that I'd never known before. I began to see life in a way that never would have been possible before. I began to relish small, daily, simple things and realized at a depth that never seemed possible that all of life was sacred. There were moments, though sporadic and far apart, when I began to understand that life wasn't over for me—but perhaps was just beginning."

BIOGRAPHICAL SKETCH

Born and raised in the inner city of Seattle, Washington, Tim was student body president and earned an award for outstanding student athlete in high school. He received a scholarship and played football and rugby at Stanford University, where he graduated from college and graduate school.

Tim is a worldwide traveler via bicycle through Europe, on a 43-foot sailboat through 25,000 miles of the Pacific Ocean, alone through Canada and the United States, and as a teacher throughout Germany, Manila, Taiwan, Japan, and New Guinea. Tim has worked as an instructor at the California Outward Bound School. He was formerly a high school teacher and a faculty member of Azusa Pacific University. His home is in LaVerne, California, with his wife, Pam, and their sons, Zac and Josh.

Believing that *"the wilderness encourages wholeness and reminds us what is true and real,"* Tim is founder and president of Summit Expedition, Inc. This mountaineering and wilderness experience school provides adventure-based educational experiences for people of all ages and backgrounds, including remarkable programs for the handicapped and delinquent youth. The program includes everything from climbing mountains, rappelling down cliffs, fording rushing mountain rivers on bridges made of two slender ropes, and surviving overnight alone.

Tim's life is filled with risk and adventure. Some years ago he taped his eyes for a good part of a week so that he was totally blind. His friend who served as his guide had him do things like go running with him, jump off a fifteen-foot tower into a lake, write a letter, and find his way out of the woods alone. Since then he has intentionally limited other senses in order to isolate and experience them.

In 1974 Tim and his friend were camping and climbing in the Sierras. Tim slipped on a snow-covered bridge, flipped over and floated almost five stories upside down, and landed on the ice at the bottom. He stood up and still made the toughest climb of the day. He made it home, but the next night he woke up with outrageous pain. He was coming out of shock. The diagnosis was that the fractures and crushed discs, on impact of the fall, had caused traumatic deteriorating arthritis. The doctor said he would have to begin to learn to live with intense pain, because it would probably be around for a lifetime. He says that the constant pain makes him sometimes feel like a butterfly that is still alive, but pinned wiggling to a board. Although Tim's constant companions are pain and fatigue, he has chosen to live his life as fully and richly as possible.

CREATIVE ENCOUNTER #1 .... Mountains and Valleys

"Joy is a process, a journey often muffled, sometimes detoured; a mystery in which we participate, not a product we can grasp."

Imagine you are on a survival training course with Tim Hansel as your instructor. You have conquered the task of surviving the wilderness challenge. Filled with wonder at the sights and sounds of nature, you wander from your group. You are alone in the Valley of the Blues, and it is starting to rain. Your teardrops fall as you find that you are lost in the dark valley of depression.

You are startled when you hear a tiny voice cheerfully saying, *"Look! The trees are shedding tears of joy and the earth's laughter. Keep singing in the rain. Climb that trail to Mount Joy. You can do it."*

You look around. Who is there? It's an incredible sight. A glistening raindrop is trying to comfort one of your teardrops.

What does a raindrop say to a teardrop? On a separate sheet of paper write about the conversation between the raindrop and your teardrop on your journey to the mountaintop. The raindrop tries to encourage the teardrop as you continue with risks and adventures to survive the drought of depression in a desert and the winter of depression in a snowstorm. The raindrop, teardrop, and you finally reach your destination, Mount Joy. As you write your story, develop the underlying meaning of the analogy that raindrops help flowers grow just as teardrops, shed due to painful experiences, help you grow.

Life is filled with happy mountaintop experiences and times of sadness in a valley. Write a few words in the valley about a sad experience, and write about a happy experience on top of the mountain.

CREATIVE ENCOUNTER #2 .... Hidden Gifts of Pain

"It has been said that there is no such thing as a problem that doesn't have a gift in it. I'm going to have to begin to find some of those gifts and open them.

"Perhaps this pain has forced some kind of awakening in me. It has established not only a new durability of the spirit and a new endurance of the heart, but also a wild and tenacious vividness of life."

A cocoon holds a butterfly captive. The struggle to be released from the cocoon is intense. If a person comes along to help the butterfly be freed more quickly, the butterfly will die, because it needs the time to fight to develop strength and poise. Little flowers may be whipped in the wind of a rainstorm, but they need the raindrops from storm clouds to grow.

Picture yourself emerging as a butterfly ready to soar freely. See yourself blossoming as a flower admired for its beauty. Your hidden gifts are being opened and developed through pain and difficulties to prepare you for even greater responsibilities in life.

Below are illustrations wrapped as gifts to represent the hidden gifts of pain. Each gift contains six steps. In each gift the first and last steps are done for you. Show the steps from the development of the cocoon to the butterfly and the growth of a flower in a gradual state of change. On another sheet of paper write about the hidden gifts of pain, that is, what you have learned and how you have changed through painful experiences.

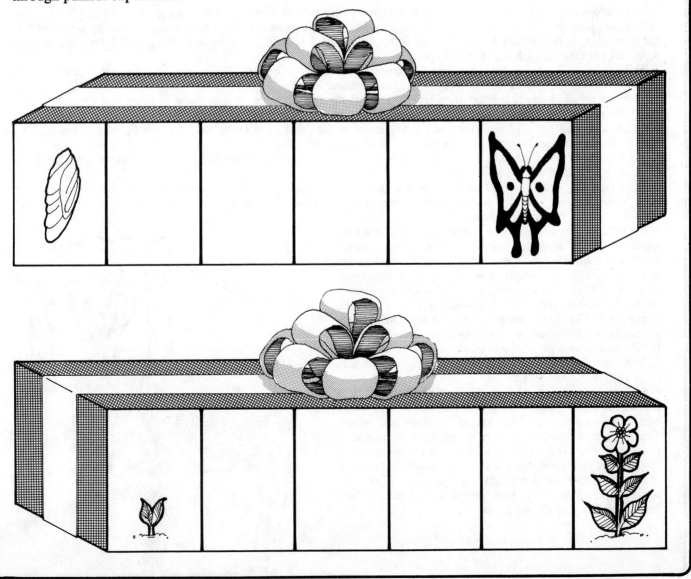

"Remember, Dad, the day they broke the news to you that you had cancer? Everyone else seemed to fall to pieces.

BUT YOU DIDN'T

"The quiet courage that you showed us all those years, sometimes when we weren't even aware of it, has shone all the more brightly these past months.

"I'm understanding, at even deeper levels, those three precious words you gave me four decades ago: 'Never Give Up.'

because . . . YOU DIDN'T!"

This is a portion of Tim's poem from his book *What Kids Need Most in a Dad*. "But You Didn't" was written just after he heard that his dad had cancer. Tim's dad died several months later.

As your teacher reads this to you, try to understand that these are painful, but normal feelings that go along with losing a loved one. You will probably be able to identify with these feelings especially if you have lost a loved one.

Reflect upon the following for discussion.

The emotional pain that comes from the news that a loved one is dying or has died is excruciating. It can be compared to feeling like a knife turning inside of you, a hundred pound weight around your neck, or like you have been hit by bricks. Your heart is so heavy. A broken spirit can cut deeply and cause extreme weariness and exhaustion. It seems that you wake up fatigued when you try to face another day with the mental anguish that death is near. Sleep may seem to be the best part of the day, for it provides escape and relief from reality. But then haunting nightmares about the death occur.

How difficult it is to see a loved one with sparkling eyes, a keen sense of humor, and abounding physical strength deteriorate right before your eyes. Even when the loved one is gone, you find yourself looking or thinking he/she is there, and then you remember in that instant he/she is gone. Tools, the smell of cookies, a toy, or a birthday card bring back pleasant memories, but then the stark reality strikes again.

Thoughts invade your mind. *"It just can't be happening, not to me. Why me? Why now? If only I would have done more? If only . . . If only . . . How can I go on and face the future without him/her?"*

A feeling of numbness and helplessness sets in. Loss of strength pervades. It may seem at times you can hardly even move, because of the heavy weight of intense emotional pain and grief. But try to take one little step at a time. Focus more on what you can do than what you cannot, more on the privilege of being alive than on the loss of energy. Lean hard on family and friends to carry you through.

The shadow of death stealthily lurks in the darkness. Death invades. The battle to live is lost. Death wounds the living. Life changes. Death teaches you how to live.

Tears flow. It's okay to cry. Teardrops are precious. Tears do not mean you are weak, but they express the strength to be you. Tears are a tender, healthy outlet of your many emotions, for you are real. Sorrow is not wasted. Tears melt away disharmony. Tears bind people closer.

Empty chairs, once filled with laughter, words of wisdom, teasing, stories of memories, talk of daily happenings, current events, and many interests are now silent. What are Thanksgiving and Christmas like with empty chairs? Empty chairs haunt you. Empty chairs invade your mind, heart, and soul. Empty chairs are lonely. To walk through the house once filled with warmth, happiness, and family gatherings and to see empty chairs create an emptiness within your heart. Empty chairs—rocking chairs, kitchen chairs, antique chairs—earthly possessions that have such sentimental value and are priceless to you are now sold at an auction or given away.

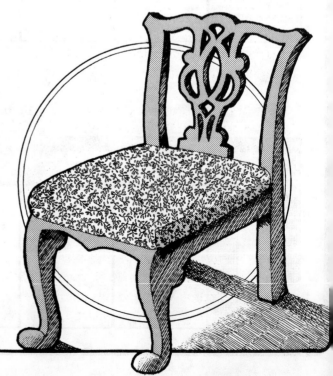

But now, ask yourself, what would your loved one who once sat in that empty chair want you to do? Yes, he/she would want you to go on with life. Pick up the pieces and go on. Time heals grief. Your broken heart mends. Love prevents scars from developing. There are golden days you will never forget. Memories of your loved one will give you strength. In the midst of death your loved one has taught you to confront life, treasure life, and learn to live. You have suffered a deep loss, but his/her influence in your life will go on.

"Joy often costs pain and suffering. It has been suggested that our cup of joy can only be as deep as our cup of sorrow."

In *Happiness Is a Choice*, Dr. Minirth and Dr. Meier discuss the grief reactions.

Stage 1: Denial. The individual refuses momentarily to believe this is really happening.

Stage 2: Anger Turned Outward. The second stage that all of us experience whenever we suffer a significant loss is an angry reaction toward someone other than ourselves. We even feel anger toward the person who died, even though he had no choice in the matter.

Stage 3: Anger Turned Inward. The grieving person begins to feel quite guilty. He has a tendency at this point to absurdly blame himself for everything. Hindsight is always better than foresight; he can see in hindsight things he could have done that may have helped prevent the loss.

Stage 4: Genuine Grief. Weeping is vitally necessary. Not grieving can lead to a low-grade depression that can last for many years.

Stage 5: Resolution. During resolution he regains his zest for life and joy. Knowing the dynamics of all five stages helps the individual to go through the five stages with less fear.

Make a collage of illustrations and words that describe your feelings about emotional pain, depression, and grief. Use velvet cloth, sandpaper, or other things to add texture to your collage. Even though it is a dark subject, try to intertwine your dark feelings with bright colors of precious memories and gleams of hope. Humor, lightness, and smiles can help relieve the heaviness of grief. At first it may be difficult to express your feelings, but try to take the first step. Expressing your grief in a creative way can help to release and heal your emotions.

*"I realized the incredible importance of making a commitment to joy. It wasn't the pain that was thwarting me as much as it was my **attitude** toward the pain. I realized that though the difficulties were undeniably real, and would remain so for the rest of my life, I had the opportunity to **choose** a new freedom and joy if I wanted to."*

Dr. Gene Getz states in *When the Pressure's On* some of the causes of depression. Depression often follows "mountaintop experiences," intense periods of stress and hyperactivity, or keen disappointment and disillusionment. Depression often coincides with physical and emotional exhaustion. Depression often results from periods of anger, particularly if we don't deal with it properly. Worry accentuates the problem and intensifies the anxiety that may have caused it in the first place. Body chemistry changes amidst depression, and the chemical imbalances are often a big part of why the depression continues. Accepting depression as a reality helps to overcome it, realizing there are reasons for its existence at this moment in our lives.

Dr. Getz gives the following practical suggestions. Check your energy level both physically and emotionally. Make sure you are getting proper physical exercise. Spend some time with someone who is not discouraged. Do something for someone else. Accomplish a task. Attempt to learn important personal lessons from difficult situations.

"Laughter adds richness, texture, and color to otherwise ordinary days. It is a gift, a choice, a discipline, and an art."

Laughter literally produces physiological and chemical changes in our bodies that bring about a greater sense of vitality and health. Tim Hansel collects everything that he can find that makes him laugh. When he speaks to groups, one of the most important elements to him is that they laugh some together.

What is the funniest moment in your life? Make up a funny story, tell about your own funny situations, or find a collection of humorous stories. Present it in front of your class. Become a comedian. Dress up as your favorite cartoon character, a clown, or other funny character for your presentation.

INDEPENDENT PROJECTS—HANSEL

1. *"When people ask which is worse, emotional pain or physical pain, I find the answer simple. Emotional pain far outweighs the other."* Compare and contrast emotional pain with physical pain. Write your thoughts about different kinds of pain. When can pain be beneficial? For example, the process of exercise, including the soreness of muscles, can work for you. What would life be like without pain?

2. *"If you can't change circumstances, change the way you respond to them."* Make a list of uncomfortable circumstances in your life. By each one indicate whether you can or cannot change it. For the ones you can change, write your plan of action to change them. For the ones you can't change, write how you plan to change your attitude toward them, just as Tim Hansel had to work through his attitude toward his constant pain.

3. *"Have we forgotten how special Wednesdays can be? Have we somehow fallen into the rut where we think that all Mondays are dreary or that February is a difficult month?"* Beat the Monday morning blues. Make a poster with humorous slogans about the positive aspects of Monday mornings, February, or how special Wednesdays can be?

4. Research outdoor survival skills. Show where you would like to hike on a story map. Include illustrations of backpacking gear and supplies you will need.

5. Create your own obstacle course. Use old tires, blindfolds, ropes, or other everyday objects. Design it to be safe, and use a stopwatch for competition. Challenge your friends to try it.

RESOURCE BOOKS—HANSEL

Bayly, Joseph. *The Last Thing We Talk About*. Elgin, Illinois: David C. Cook Publishing Co., 1973.

Coutellier, Connie. *Outdoor Book*. Kansas City, Missouri: Camp Fire, Inc., 1980.

Hansel, Tim. *Holy Sweat*. Waco, Texas: Word Books, 1987.

_____. *You Gotta Keep Dancin'*. Elgin, Illinois: David C. Cook Publishing Co., 1985.

_____. *What Kids Need Most in a Dad*. Old Tappan, New Jersey: Fleming H. Revell Co., 1984.

_____. *When I Relax I Feel Guilty*. Elgin, Illinois: David C. Cook Publishing Co., 1979.

Knap, Jerome J. *The Complete Outdoorsman's Handbook: A Guide to Outdoor Living and Wilderness Survival*. Toronto: Pagurian Press Limited, 1974.

Krementz, Jill. *How It Feels When a Parent Dies*. New York: Alfred A. Knopf, 1981.

LeShan, Eda. *Learning to Say Good-By: When a Parent Dies*. New York: Macmillan Publishing Co., Inc., 1976.

Minirth, Frank B., and Paul D. Meier. *Happiness Is a Choice: A Manual on the Symptoms, Causes, and Cures of Depression*. Richardson, Texas: Today Publishers, Inc., 1978.

Richards, Larry, and Paul Johnson. *Death & the Caring Community: Ministering to the Terminally Ill*. Portland, Oregon: Multnomah Press, 1980.

Tatelbaum, Judy. *The Courage to Grieve: Creative Living, Recovery, and Growth Through Grief*. New York: Harper & Row, 1980.

WALK FROM THE PAST TO THE FUTURE

CAROLYN KOONS

"Looking in the mirror again, I saw past my reflection into my own childhood. Memories, so vivid I could smell, feel, taste them, stabbed at my heart. Why was this happening? I rarely looked back at my childhood. I had walked away from all that ugliness; it was not relevant to my life today. But there it was, my own past, flashing before my eyes in the mirror, as if I were drowning. It was eerie!

"My dad constantly reeking of alcohol, his violent anger constantly raging; my baby brother lying in a pool of blood; my mother standing over me with a loaded gun; my sixth grade teacher telling me that I was no good; shooting up vacant cabins with my friends just to prove we really didn't care and that maybe, just maybe, we were bad just like everyone seemed to think.

"Love heals wounds, erases scars, sets a foundation, and builds a future. Every day I worked hard to turn my life around, putting the bad behind and building the good into my life."

BIOGRAPHICAL SKETCH

Carolyn's parents treated her two brothers one way and her another. What happened to Carolyn or how she felt didn't matter to any of them. Her father gave her a junkyard bike, while her brothers got the best. For three long days on their trip to California her father forced her to sit in a tiny space on a cold wooden piano bench in their van, while her brothers had the comfort of mattresses.

Her father was an alcoholic, and his violent anger constantly raged. After threats upon her life, Carolyn lived with the fear that her father would kill her. Thirteen-year-old Carolyn resented her mother for dumping the responsibility of managing their motel in Crescent, Oregon, on her. Due to her father's job on a railroad construction crew, her family moved seven times in less than a year. At the age of fourteen, her family abandoned her in Minnesota.

Living in a depressed fantasy world, Carolyn diverted to vandalism, stealing, drinking, and playing hooky from school. Through the upheavals, the repeated threats and painful rejections, she faced more loneliness and fear than she could bear, until she was befriended by a woman, who invited her to church and introduced her to friends who deeply cared for her. Soon the same Carolyn who had spent her early teen years nearly destroying her life was helping a junior high group do fun, constructive things.

The young coed, who could only read at an eighth grade level before she entered college, graduated from Azusa Pacific University with a high grade point average and was honored as a member of that year's Who's Who Among College Students in America. She is a professor of education and founding director for the Institute of Outreach Ministries at Azusa Pacific University in southern California. Along with four other faculty members, she was named Outstanding Educator in America.

Carolyn rescued Antonio, a child incarcerated in a Mexican prison since the age of five on a trumped-up murder charge. Carolyn's investigations led her into a two-and-a-half year legal battle, a web of conflicting stories, bureaucratic red tape, and a frustrating legal system which acknowledged that the boy must be innocent but refused to release him. Finally Tony found himself with a new mother and a new life. Tony was the same imprisoned, angry, terrified, lonely child that she had been—a prisoner of the painful past. Together they inched away from the despair of struggling to forget the past and stepped forward to live in the present with an added purpose to use their past experiences to help others.

"A few twinkling stars seen from my window shone as very small beacons of hope. I could neither sleep nor banish the pain while the day replayed moment by excruciating moment. My chest tightened even a notch more with loneliness until I wanted to cry, but couldn't."

Imagine the excitement and thrill of a ride on a roller coaster. The safety bar snaps shut, and you are locked inside the car of "Motion Mania." You hold the bar in a white-knuckle grip. You can hardly wait to begin, but at the same time, you're almost choking with fear. The roller coaster accelerates at a breathtaking speed, whipping you up and down in dips and turns.

Before you can take another breath, you are launched upside down into a high loop. After you've completed the loop, you are right side up again, rising to a high incline. It pauses at the top. As you look down, you scream with anticipation. Here comes the ultimate plunge. It's over. You stagger from the ride, feeling light-headed, nevertheless, happy to have both feet on the ground.

Think of a time when your emotions were like a roller coaster. You wanted to be in control; but exciting events, unforeseen circumstances, the fear of the unknown, and disappointments swirled you to experience the heights and depths of emotions. Intellectually, you wanted to go one way, but your intense emotions swayed you to another. The motion of the runaway emotions churned inside of you. By the end of the emotional ride, you coasted to a state of dizziness and numbness.

Sometimes we can just freely enjoy our emotions. Other times we need to feel free to express our emotions without criticism or anyone trying to stifle our emotions. Moreover, time is often needed to heal our damaged emotions. The quest is to take control and channel our emotions constructively before they run away or before they cripple relationships. In other words, we need to somehow try to control our emotions, rather than let our emotions control us.

In a class discussion talk about destructive and constructive ways to handle or control emotions. Discuss the characteristics of following emotions: anger, depression, envy, grief, guilt, impatience, inferiority, infatuation, loneliness, shyness, worry or fear. Here is an example, as a guide for the format of your discussion. What is anger like? Anger is like an erupting volcano. What are destructive ways to handle anger? Throw sarcastic insults, repress it, display the silent treatment, antagonize your little brother, kick a big rock. What are constructive ways to handle anger? Count to ten to slow down the erupting volcano, punch pillows, confront the offender, forgive and forget, kick a football.

Try to put the constructive ways into action. After a short period of time, reunite in a discussion to share some of your successes and failures in trying to handle your emotions.

CREATIVE ENCOUNTER #2 .... "E"motion Pictures

Follow this series of motion pictures that depict the stages of rejection. First, you experience high hopes and expectations of a budding relationship, as represented in the bubble. You decide to take a risk and put your heart out on a limb. Rejection hits. Your hopes are dashed. The bubble is burst, and your heart is shattered into many pieces. Consequently, you have to make a choice. Withdraw and build a wall around yourself to protect yourself from any further risk of rejection. Or bounce back from the rejection and try again.

Draw a series of motion pictures to represent the stages of an emotion. Ask a friend to figure out what emotion you have portrayed and see if he can describe the stages of your "e"motion pictures.

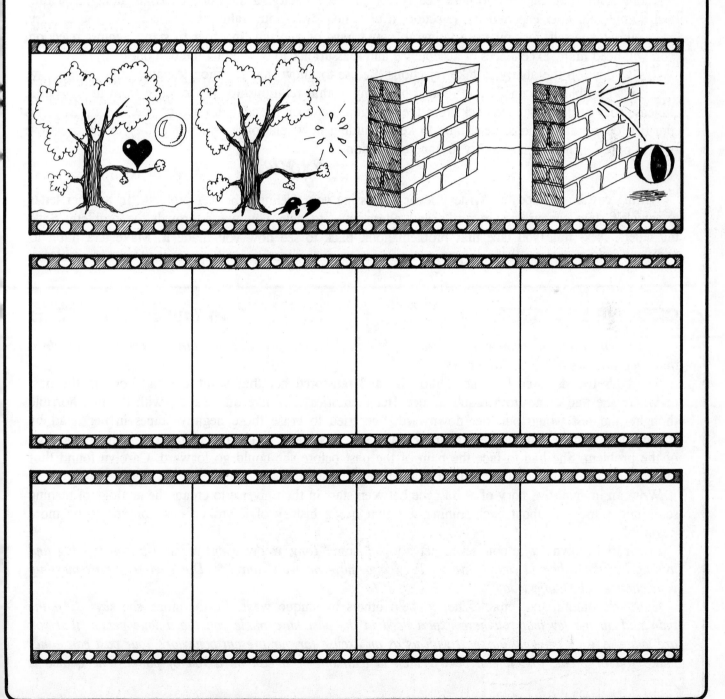

"The emptiness of rejection was being replaced by committed friendships."

Dear Hope,

I have been rejected by someone that meant a lot to me, and let me tell you how I feel. Rejection is like an ocean of love smashed against the rocks. It almost seems like I am being punished for caring. The pain is gripping like a load of emotional bricks crashing upon my heart. The intensity of the shocking pain seems to immobilize my fragile emotions, to paralyze my hopes and dreams. Please give me your advice to help me work through this.

Dashed Hopes

Dear Dashed Hopes,

Along with your capacity to care deeply comes the capacity to hurt deeply. Even though you may feel humiliated, after experiencing rejection, it does not lower your value as a person. Yet you can feel good about yourself, for you were vulnerable and gave of yourself. In order to stand against rejection, you will need many experiences of acceptance and reassurance to counteract the bad ones.

Try to develop the ability to take rejections. Refuse to allow that rejection to cause you to withdraw. See if it's possible to reconcile and rebuild harmony in that relationship. Try to learn from the rejection. Release the rejection. Bounce back from the rejection. Lean on friends who accept you. Even if it means the risk of more rejections, determine to keep building new relationships. Your ability to discover love will in part depend on your ability to handle rejection.

Hope

Writing can be therapeutic. Write a letter expressing your feelings about a problem. In another letter to yourself state encouraging remarks and alternatives to help you work through the problem. Save the letters. Next time you face that problem, look back to see how you made it. Make it a habit to pen your feelings and see them on paper to give you new perspectives and approaches to your problems.

"As I looked out the window at the gray night and the stars sprinkled through the heavens, I imagined that each was one of my healed memories."

Carolyn's friends loved her unconditionally and reassured her that what she had done in the past or where she had come from didn't matter. Her memories were like quicksand—with the first horrible thought, the rest would pull her downward. She tried to erase those negative tapes in her head by staying busy, but the tapes kept playing. Finally she was ready to go to the starting point, to the root of the problem. She had to face the pain of the past before she could go forward. Carolyn found that foregiveness lies at the heart of all inner healing.

Write an imaginative story of a dialogue between stars in the universe to create the analogy of turning scars into stars. Tell about each shining star that has a history of a broken past, broken to be more beautiful.

Listen to Carolyn's wise counsel to her adopted son. *"Tony, you've spent years in prison fighting and hitting, but that's behind you. Leave it, Tony, and move on with your life. Don't let your past mess up your chance to be happy today!"*

Carolyn's painful past enables her to help others in unique ways. Furthermore, she says, *"All the pain and all the joy that you have experienced in the past have made you the unique person that you are today. Are we bringing our past with us as an excuse for our present behavior? Your past can either make you or break you. It can be a crutch to lean on, or it can be a rod of power. The choice is yours."*

CREATIVE ENCOUNTER #5 ....A Tapestry of Your Life

"Healing brought newness to my life. My season of running from my past slowly came to a halt, turning into a time of inner springtime. The newly plowed soil of my heart was prepared for sowing. The seeds of added purpose and challenge seemed to be dropped daily into my life."

The patchwork pattern in Carolyn's life took on new meaning. Her experiences turned into a beautiful tapestry in her heart and mind as memories became the key to her future.

Tapestry is a fabric woven with yarns of various colors to form a picture or an ornamental design. The tapestry weaver faces the back of the fabric as he works.

Reflect for a moment about the mosaic in your life. Draw a pattern, intertwining a hodgepodge of colors, on the underside of a tapestry to represent difficult experiences and memories of your past. Now turn the fabric over, and visualize the other side of the tapestry. Draw pictures, especially using nature, to illustrate your life on the front of the tapestry. Label both sides of the tapestry. What meaning can you see in your past and present experiences? Your memories, both painful and pleasant, can be interwoven into a beautiful tapestry to prepare you for the greater challenges of our future.

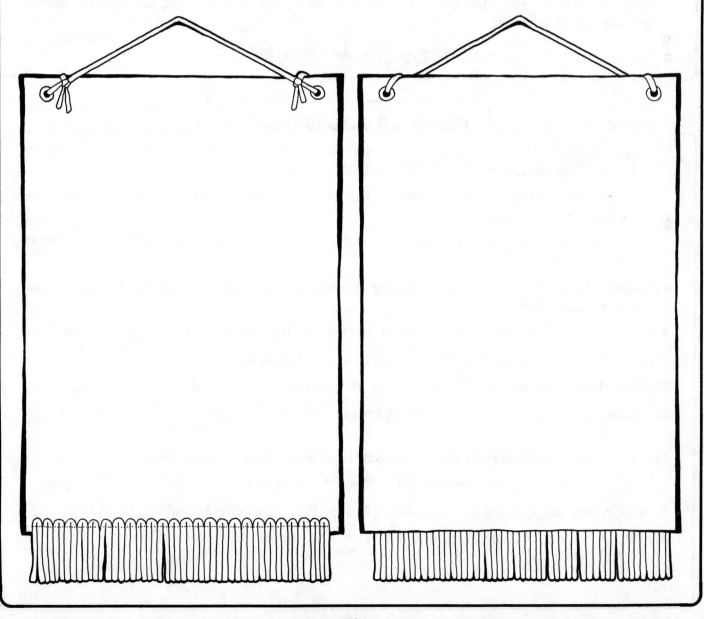

INDEPENDENT PROJECTS—KOONS

1. *"As a child I did everything I could to earn love and acceptance. I wasn't very successful, so I changed my tactics; the more rejection I felt, the worse I behaved. It was just as though I'd decided that if my world treated me as if I were bad, I'd show them what bad really meant. In time, all I knew was how to get into trouble. Inside, I was really lonely, and my frantic search for comfort constantly got me in trouble."* Read case studies and research the causes of and reactions to emotions. Include guidelines to appropriately handle different emotions.

2. *"My hurt turned to anger."* In *The Friendship Factor*, Dr. Alan Loy McGinnis offers five techniques to help you get angry without becoming destructive. 1. Talk about your feelings, not your friend's faults. 2. Stick to one topic. 3. Allow your friend to respond. 4. Aim for ventilation, not conquest. 5. Balance criticism with lots of affection. Make up a skit about two people who are angry with each other. Present it to your class to demonstrate how these techniques successfully resolved their conflict.

3. Refer to *Harry Lorayne's Page-A-Minute Memory Book*. Use the link system, as described in this book, to give a speech to your class about techniques to improve memory skills.

4. Sharpen your mental images. Make a collection of several items on a tray. Pass the tray around the room. Then remove the tray of items, and challenge your classmates to write every item down on paper. Another possibility is for you and a friend to take a walk. Then ask detailed, specific questions about colors, etc.

RESOURCE BOOKS—KOONS

Carlson, Dwight L. *Overcoming Hurts and Anger: How to Identify and Cope with Negative Emotions.* Eugene, Oregon: Harvest House Publishers, 1981.

Carter, Les. *Good 'n' Angry: How to Handle Your Anger Positively.* Grand Rapids, Michigan: Baker Book House, 1983.

_____ . *Mind over Emotions: How to Mentally Control Your Feelings.* Grand Rapids, Michigan: Baker Book House, 1985.

Coleman, William L. *Bouncing Back: Finding Acceptance in the Face of Rejection.* Eugene, Oregon: Harvest House Publishers, 1985.

Koons, Carolyn A. *Beyond Betrayal: Healing My Broken Past.* San Francisco: Harper & Row, 1986.

_____ . *Tony: Our Journey Together.* San Francisco: Harper & Row, 1984.

Lorayne, Harry. *Harry Lorayne's Page-A-Minute Memory Book.* New York: Ballantine Books, 1985.

McGinnis, Alan Loy. *Confidence: How to Succeed at Being Yourself.* Minneapolis: Augsburg Publishing House, 1987.

Seamonds, David A. *Healing for Damaged Emotions.* Wheaton, Illinois: Victor Books, 1981.

_____ . *Healing of Memories.* Wheaton, Illinois: Victor Books, 1985.

Reagan, Nancy, and Jane Wilkie. *To Love a Child.* New York: The Bobbs-Merrill Co., Inc., 1982.

Wright, H. Norman. *Making Peace with Your Past.* Old Tappan, New Jersey: Fleming H. Revell Co., 1985.

WALK FROM DISAPPROVAL TO INTEGRITY

ERIC LIDDELL

"Here are some questions to ask yourself. If I know something to be true, am I prepared to follow it even though it is contrary to what I want, to what I have previously said or held to be true? Will I follow it even if it means loss of face, owning that I was wrong? Will I follow if it means being laughed at by friend or foe, if it means personal financial loss or some kind of hardship?

"Following truth leads to God, for truth is of God. Obedience is the secret of being conscious that God guides you personally. If in the quiet of your heart you feel something should be done, stop and consider whether it is in line with the character and teaching of Jesus. If it is, obey that impulse to do it, and in doing so you will find it was God guiding you."

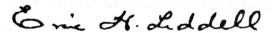

BIOGRAPHICAL SKETCH

In 1902 Eric was born to Scottish missionaries in a China humiliated and torn by foreign intervention. They were surrounded by murders and horrible persecutions. Eric, his brother Robert and sister Jenny spent a lot of time playing with Chinese children. Rob, age eight, and Eric, not yet seven, were sent to the School for the Sons of Missionaries in London. Not only could he run, but most sports came easily to Eric. At school Eric was popular, and he became captain of both cricket and rugby.

Eric attended Edinburgh University, and he was on their team for the Scottish Inter-University Sports. He broke records and brought home trophies and prizes from national and international meetings. Contrary to the impression suggested by *Chariots of Fire*, there was never any opposition from his family to his athletics. They were all thrilled about his running.

Eric was known for his chivalry on the racetrack, such as shaking hands with his opponents before the race. In the Triangular Contest with England and Ireland, Eric represented Scotland and won all three sprints—the 100, the 220 and the 440 yards. In the 440 yards Eric was forced off the track onto the grass. The opponents were twenty yards ahead of him. Arms swinging, fists punching the air, head thrown back, he passed everyone and won. He collapsed in exhaustion at the tape.

In the 1924 Olympics in Paris, Eric refused to run the 100 meters on Sunday due to his convictions. He ran in the 400 meters instead and won the gold medal. When Eric stepped quietly out of the limelight a year later to serve as a missionary in China, crowds of people came to say good-bye to him. For a number of years he taught science at the Anglo-Chinese College in Tientsin and then decided to tackle the task of reaching people in the rural areas, traveling many miles in rugged conditions by foot and bicycle.

As conditions in China deteriorated in the weeks before the bombing of Pearl Harbor, Eric arranged for his family to leave China, planning to be with them a few months later. His wife gave birth to their third daughter, whom Eric never saw. Before he could leave, the Japanesse armies rounded up all the enemy nationals and placed them in an internment camp. Eric organized sports and recreation, helped people by teaching and tutoring, and was responsible for keeping law and order in the camp. Eric cared for the prisoners with such devotion that his own health suffered. When he died from a brain tumor in camp in 1945, Scotland received the news with a feeling of shock and a universal sense of loss.

CREATIVE ENCOUNTER #1 . . . . A Sports Hero

"It was the genuine power of his personality that drew people, the compulsion of his belief, the down-to-earth quality of his sincerity. For children and adults alike adored Eric Liddell. Eric's great secret was that he loved people, and could talk to anyone."

A fourteen-year-old schoolgirl started the Eric Liddell Fan Club. The teenage members were instructed to live upright lives and *"always uphold Eric Liddell."*

Choose one of your favorite sports heroes. Write a statement about his/her life philosophy or life motto in the baseball bat, how he/she overcame adversity in the football, his/her achievements in the basketball, and words of recognition and praise for your sports hero on the trophy.

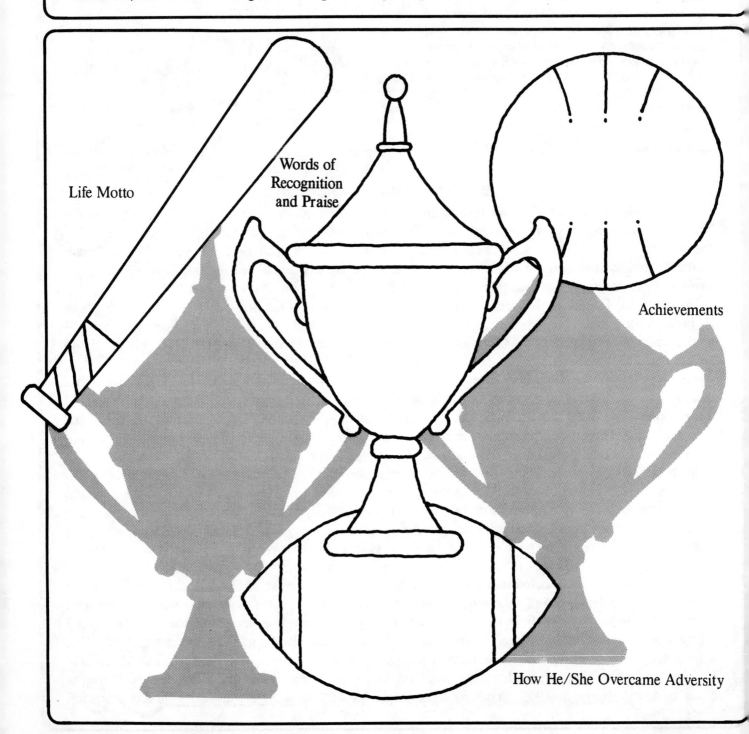

Life Motto

Words of Recognition and Praise

Achievements

How He/She Overcame Adversity

CREATIVE ENCOUNTER #2 ....My Name

"He had the common touch, the ability to talk to anyone like a friend and make that person feel both important and challenged. That must be why no one who recalls even the most fleeting contact with Eric Liddell has anything less than the most fulsome tribute to pay to him."

Eric Liddell's name and reputation were held in high regard, and his influence and his stand for his principles live on. Work to uphold a good reputation that will reflect the worth of your name.

Care must be taken to respect and protect another person's name and reputation. Calling people nicknames, especially that focus on a negative aspect of another person, can cause deep pain, even though they might smile politely. Unique characteristics can become the titles of people, such as someone who is extra tall may be called "Gigantic Giant." That person may already be self-conscious about his height, and calling attention to it in a mocking manner could hurt another's self-esteem.

Be proud of your name. Living a life that honors and protects your family's name is of utmost importance.

Find the meaning of your name. Use *The Name Book* or other books about the meanings of names as references. Observe, study, and practice various styles of calligraphy. *The Complete Book of Calligraphy* or other books about calligraphy located in the library will help you develop various styles of calligraphy. Write your name and the meaning of your name in calligraphy.

CREATIVE ENCOUNTER #3 . . . . Standing Alone

"Quietly, he just said, 'I'm not running on a Sunday.' He captured the imagination of millions by tossing away his chance of a gold medal in the 100 meters—the race he was a favorite to win—because a principle of his Christian faith mattered more. When he unexpectedly won the 400 meters instead, the country was at his feet."

Eric was Britain's main hope for the 100 meters, and the British athletic authorities were horrified. Eric was called a traitor to his country which deeply hurt him. Harold Abrahams, the son of a Lithuanian Jew, ran this race and was the first European to win the 100 meters. Before the 400-meter race Eric received a note of encouragement. It read: *"In the old book it says, He that honours me I will honour. Wishing you the best of success always."* When he won the Olympic title, newspapers which had once called him a "traitor" now lauded him.

Close your eyes. As your teacher reads the following, imagine yourself in a situation similar to Eric Liddell's experience in his stand for his principles. Then discuss your "gold medal," the symbolism of your "gold medal," the "cracks in your gold medal," compromise, and dreams.

Fight for Your Dreams

Have you ever wondered what you would do in a *Chariots of Fire* situation? You have worked hard for your dream to come true. You are given an unbelievable offer. This is the opportunity you have been waiting for; the door is wide open. It's like everything is handed to you on a silver platter. It's that "gold medal!" You've worked for it. Go for it! It's yours.

All of a sudden, you look closely, and you see cracks in that gold medal. Those cracks represent compromise. Your hand is open, ready to accept that gold medal—your dream.

Stop! Those cracks could shatter that medal. The consequences of compromise could shatter your life. You are disappointed and disillusioned. If you do not accept that gold medal, you will lose hours of work that prepared you for that moment, money, and possible fame. Your dream will be crushed. The cracks in the gold medal are getting bigger and bigger. But you want it. Can you live with yourself, accept the gold medal, and compromise your principles?

Remember you are accountable to others. You close your hand and watch the gold medal shatter into many pieces. You may have lost hours of work, money, and fame, but you did not lose your self-respect. You did what you believed in.

You ask yourself, "How can doing right hurt so badly?" It can hurt to stand alone. But look up! The Olympic torch is still burning. There will be other opportunities. You stood for what is right. You can feel proud for doing what is right. Wait and you will reap the harvest. A new solid gold medal with no cracks will come your way. Fight for your new hopes and dreams. Your dreams will come true with no compromise.

CREATIVE ENCOUNTER #4 .... Role Playing

Know what you believe in and stand up for it. It is essential to have made the decision of where you stand on various issues before you enter those situations. At the time of a tempting situation, it may look like fun, so you need to absolutely know where you stand beforehand. Know yourself. Know what has a negative pull on you. Discuss the pressures with others. Ask your parents, teachers, and friends to help you. Be accountable to others. Learn to say no. Be strong and discipline yourself to follow through on your convictions. Stand firmly. Be true to yourself.

Role playing these situations will help to prepare you to think about where you stand on these issues. Ask yourself these questions: Where do I stand on these issues? What would I do if I were in this situation? How would I respond? What are the alternatives? How will I handle peer pressure?

You might want to try different approaches or switch parts. Make a list of alternatives and responses. Put yourself in the situation and try to concentrate on building wise decision-making skills. Practice your role playing, and then perform in front of your group.

Your peers are jealous that you and your close friend make good grades. You have both been called, "Brain," "Teacher's Pet," "Goody, Goody," and "Bookworm." You enjoy reading, school, and learning, but yet you want to fit in and not feel different. Your close friend feels desperate to be accepted and decides to purposefully miss a few answers on the test and makes a C. Then you see they make fun of your close friend because she made a C and did not get an A, as she usually does. You perceive that your friend and you are teased for being good students, and when your friend thought she could fit in by making a C, she was also teased. You and your friend get together to discuss a seemingly no-win situation. To add to your dilemma, your friends are pushing you to take more time with them, which will take away from finishing your homework. How will you balance your time? Will you continue to do your best no matter what others say? Talk about who is teasing you, why they are teasing you, and how it is affecting you.

You are popular and looked upon as a leader in your class. Your classmates respect you, and you often notice they follow what you do. Your dream is to become class president. You have worked hard for this position. You are preparing your campaign speech. You want to impress your friends so much to persuade them to vote for you that you find yourself thinking of heroic stories about yourself that are stretching the truth, and you want to promise high expectations for the class that seem unattainable. It will be a close race with your opponent. You are trying to decide whether to "color" your speech with exaggeration to impress your friends or just take a risk and be yourself. Actually prepare a campaign speech for your class.

A dream come true—you are chosen for the team. You have worked out for hours and days, practiced, and exercised. But there is one drawback; your grades in one of your classes have progressively gone down. You have studied, but you are so nervous about failing this crucial test. You feel the teammates' pressure, because they need you on the team. One of your teammates approaches you with a way to cheat that seems safe; that is, no one will probably find out you have cheated. This test is a turning point for you. If you pass it, you make the team. If not, you will be off the team for six weeks. What will you do to pass this test? How can you improve your study skills to help you feel more confident that you can pass the test? Will you ask your teacher and coach for extra help to pass the test? Talk over the alternatives with your friend.

CREATIVE ENCOUNTER #5 ....Dare to Be Different

"Sheep are said to be the most habitual animals known to man. They love to play follow-the-leader. A sheep will do whatever the other sheep are doing. Whole herds of sheep have been known to wander into disaster and even fall off the side of a cliff, because they were blindly playing follow-the-leader.

"When we play follow-the-leader and do only what is safe and free from ridicule, we, too, might well wander off the side of some cliff and plunge to destruction. We need to be careful because the games we often play are dangerous," states Fred Hartley in his book *Dare to Be Different.*

Draw an illustration of the sheep or think of another analogy or situation that depicts the consequences of peer pressure. Make a script for your *Chariots of Fire* situation. Write words of advice to counteract the pressure on your illustration.

CREATIVE ENCOUNTER #6 ....Fighting for Principles

Eric risked his own life to fight against the dangers to preserve the lives of others. In the internment camp in China, Eric heard about a wounded man who was dying, and none of the local people dared to help for fear of the Japanese. Despite the fear of the consequences, Eric persuaded a workman to accompany him with his cart to rescue the wounded man. While they were in the midst of encircling troops, they heard of another seriously injured man. Eric and his companion reached the dying man, placed him in the cart, and walked both desperately wounded men eighteen miles farther to the mission hospital.

Make a list of at least five things you consider worth fighting for: your beliefs, your family, your country, your dreams, etc. Now make another list of at least five things you consider aren't worth fighting for: your brand of toothpaste, the color of your skateboard, the number of times you can jump rope, etc.

Compare the lists. What do you find? You will discover the first list contains major items, while the ones on the second list are relatively minor. Pick one item worth fighting for, and make your stand known today by spoken word or written letter. Address your thoughts about your principles in an imaginary letter to Eric Liddell. Convictions worth having are worth communicating.

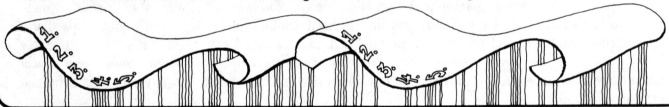

CREATIVE ENCOUNTER #7.................................A Character Study

"In his work in China he created an opportunity for the talents with which he was so richly endowed— courage, determination, skill, endurance, and self-sacrifice—to be utilized to the fullest. Sport gave to Eric Liddell its highest honours; nevertheless, it is true to say that he honoured sport rather than sport honouring him."

Principles, like keeping the seventh day of the week holy as a day of rest, had been instilled into Eric from boyhood. He listened, he accepted, and then like the perfectionist he was, he worked on it until his beliefs became a part of his mind and personality.

Ian Charleson, who played Eric in *Chariots of Fire*, admired his serenity. Sally Magnusson, the author of his biography, was struck by his consistency.

Cite the parts of *The Flying Scotsman* where people talk about their memories of Eric. Do a character study of Eric Liddell. Make a list of his qualities and give examples of how these character traits and his life influenced others.

CREATIVE ENCOUNTER #8 ....Handling Peer Pressure

How can doing right hurt so badly? Often it can be painful when you stand for what is right. There is no responsibility without accountability. Doing what is right can mean giving up a dream you have worked for, loss of hours of work, loss of friends or money, mocking, or rejection. But the benefits are lasting.

Compromise and not standing for what is right can also have painful consequences. Compromise can mean loss of self-respect, disappointing and hurting people, and devastating consequences. You may have the pride and acceptance of your peers, or no one may know you compromised, but you have to live with the thoughts of not being true to yourself.

You may have to stand alone. No one may notice or praise you for your stand. In fact, it may seem that the others who did compromise are having fun and reaping the rewards. It may look like there are no benefits for doing what is right, or there may be bountiful rewards or new opportunities. Concerned people will help you in difficult decisions, but you make the ultimate choice. You may have to make the choice: self-respect or peer rejection. Think about it. The choice is yours.

How can we handle peer pressure? Gary R. Collins, author of *Give Me a Break!* suggests the following steps.

Expect the pressure so that it doesn't come as a surprise.
Resist the pressure with the help of real friends.
Counteract the pressure, replacing it with something better.
Avoid the pressure, whenever this is possible.
Get up and start over, whenever you give in to the pressure.

What are some of the helpful pressures you've experienced? How have you become better through them? What were some of the harmful pressures placed on you? How did you respond? How have you felt peer pressure from the media? Is it easier to be yourself, or is it easier to compromise? When you give in to peer pressure, how do you feel? What are reasons that people give in to peer pressure? What strategies do you plan to use to fight peer pressure? What would you do in a *Chariots of Fire* situation?

CREATIVE ENCOUNTER #9 ....Taking a Stand

"The question of what the 1980's would make of Eric Liddell led me on to another: what would Eric Liddell make of the 1980's? Could he ever have become a world record-breaker today and still have fulfilled the commitments to his faith and the sharing of it that were so important to him? Would there have been the same joy in running, the same throwing back of the head in the sheer exultation of the race, if he had had to submit to the rigours and the professionalism and the extraordinarily exacting standards of sport today? More to the point, could he ever have got away with the quiet announcement of his refusal to run on a Sunday that so impressed his peers, or the uncomplicated decision to slip away from stardom to be a missionary on the other side of the world?"

Sally Magnusson asked these questions in her biography about Eric Liddell. What do you think Eric would do today? Answer these questions in an essay, and include comparisons of the sports world in Eric's lifetime to the contemporary world of sports.

1. Watch the film *Chariots of Fire*. Find interesting facts about Eric's life in China, such as the following episode. Eric was scheduled in a race in North China just half an hour before his boat was due to leave to take him back to college. Eric won the race, and a waiting taxi rushed him to the docks. By this time the boat was already moving out from the dock. When a wave momentarily lifted the boat nearer, Eric threw his bags on board and took a leap, managing to land on the back of the moving boat. Write a movie script about Eric's life after the Olympics. Choose actors for your script and present your "movie" to the class.

2. Make a chart of peer pressures. Basically peer pressures can be divided into three influences: good, neutral, and bad influences. Think of how you have handled these pressures in the past. Write on the chart how you plan to respond to each of those pressures.

3. *"A Cunningham never quits,"* I'd heard my father say often to us children. *"Pain, hard work, tough times, little money, we can stand anything."* Burned severely in a school fire, Glenn Cunningham at age seven was told he would never walk again. In 1936 he won the silver Olympic medal in the 1500-meter race. In 1979 Glenn was selected as the outstanding track performer of the century of Madison Square Garden's history. Cite examples in his life that show the Cunningham's family philosophy of "Never Quit."

4. Research the training programs of Olympic stars. If you were a coach of an Olympic champion, what schedule and exercise program would you plan for him/her? Design this program.

Antonacci, Robert J., and Gene Schoor. *Track and Field for Young Champions*. New York: McGraw-Hill Book Co., 1974.

Austin, Dorothea. *The Name Book*. Minneapolis: Bethany House Publishers, 1982.

Butterworth, Emma Macalik. *The Complete Book of Calligraphy*. New York: Lippincott & Crowell Publishers, 1980.

Collins, Gary R. *Give Me a Break!* Old Tappan, New Jersey: Fleming H. Revell Co., 1984.

Cunningham, Glenn, and George X. Sand. *Never Quit*. Lincoln, Virginia: Chosen Books Publishing Co., Ltd., 1981.

Giller, Norman. *The 1984 Olympics Handbook*. New York: Holt, Rinehart and Winston, 1983.

Greenberg, Stan. *The Guinness Book of Olympics: Facts and Feats*. New York: Sterling Publishing Co., Inc., 1983.

Hartley, Fred. *Dare to Be Different: Dealing with Peer Pressure*. Old Tappan, New Jersey: Fleming H. Revell Co., 1980.

Liddell, Eric. *The Disciplines of the Christian Life*. Nashville, Tennessee: Abingdon Press, 1985.

Lutes, Chris. *Peer Pressure: Making It Work for You!* Wheaton, Illinois: Tyndale House Publisher, Inc., 1987.

Magnusson, Sally. *The Flying Scotsman*. New York: Quartet Books, Inc., 1981.

Wallechinsky, David. *The Complete Book of the Olympics*. New York: Penguin Books, 1984.

WALK FROM BROKENNESS TO HAPPINESS

ART LINKLETTER

"I do not think that happiness is a clever television script or a five thousand dollar check or a top-ranking show. It is not the vanquishing of a rival, nor your name in a column, nor a house with a pool.

"To me, happiness is like a play that has lightness and darkness, motion and sound—and a heart. It is a baby's plaintive cry at night, and I have heard it often. It is the laughter of a child discovering the good things in the world, and I am blessed with such laughter every day of my life. It is the gentle, reassuring touch of Lois' hand when trouble darkens our days. It is the sensitive, appealing letter from a foster child in some distant land—and I have four such wards—telling us what keeps him going, the knowledge that he is loved and needed by someone.

"Happiness is a word of praise for work well-done, or an enriching hour with a friend, time gained in the race of life. It is a family like mine—together on a camping trip high in the mountains, or at a picnic at the beach. Our family is a unit in an adventure of living, and an experiment in love. It has never failed."

BIOGRAPHICAL SKETCH

When Art was only a few months old, his natural parents gave him up for adoption in Moose Jaw, a small town in Canada's Saskatchewan province. Living on the ragged edge of poverty, his foster father decided to move to San Diego in search of a way to support the three of them.

In grammar school Art had two favorite after-school pastimes, playing basketball and giving speeches. No one guided Art in the proper direction with his speaking ability, so he did it on his own. After class, he would often go to the school auditorium and give speeches to imaginary audiences. Later, in high school and college, he specialized in chairing assemblies, leading debating teams, and acting as student liaison to service organizations.

Art finished high school a month before he was sixteen and set out to see the world. With ten dollars in his pocket and his parents' blessing, he hitchhiked, rode freight trains, and worked in almost every state in the Union. He sailed out of New York on a ship and worked his way to Buenos Aires and back.

Upon his return home, Art enrolled in San Diego State College, where he studied to be a teacher of voice and dramatics. His ability to talk extemporaneously led him to work as an announcer in his junior year for station KGB San Diego. Art had settled on teaching as an occupation. Unexpectedly, he was offered a job working at a local radio station for $5 more than the teaching job would have paid. He accepted the offer. His ultimate goal of speaking to people, influencing them through his oral presentations, remained the same, but the path to that goal had changed dramatically. In 1942 Art moved to Hollywood and soon began his popular shows.

America knows and loves Art as the warmhearted host of *People Are Funny* and *House Party*—two of the longest-running shows in broadcasting history. He has enjoyed international acclaim as a radio and television performer, a best-selling author, an astute businessman, and a popular lecturer. Art and his wife Lois had five children.

While Art was never actually hungry or neglected, his childhood was a little austere and lonely. The absence of a normal home life acted on him as a spur. He wanted to go places, meet people, make money, achieve security, and find warmth, companionship, and love. He found all these things. Furthermore, Art has given people in a needy world a friendly smile, laughter, and genuine love.

"Art himself retains the lively spirit and zest of youth which have made a legion of kids confide in him and regard him as a special friend," said Walt Disney.

Art looks at life through a wonderful window—the eyes of a child. As we grow up, we often wear blinders and just narrowly focus on the commonplace of everyday life. Remember as a small child how you could magically turn a sheet into a tent or transform a broom into a horse. Keep your imaginative flights and inventive curiosity alive. Art encourages us to always see the wonders of life through the eyes of a child.

Art's spontaneous wit and humor, as he interviewed children on his *House Party* show, have entertained millions. Enjoy these quips inspired by Art on his program. Wander into the world of childlike wonderment with Art and his "kids."

After you have laughed awhile, choose a few of these quips and illustrate them in cartoons. Keep a treasured diary of quotes from your family members. Make up a title, like "Benjamin's Babblings," which could be the title of a diary of your little brother's quotes.

A practical pet was dreamed up by a seven-year-old girl who said she'd like most of all to have a beaver for a chum. When I remarked on such an odd choice, she said:*"No, it isn't. He could sharpen my pencils for me."*

Some kids aren't content with the usual dog or cat. They branch out into menageries, like the boy who said:

"I have three guinea pigs, two dogs and a sick turkey."

"What's wrong with the turkey?"

"He's got the chicken pox."

"What do you want to be?"

"A football player."

"What position?"

"Third base."

An older child with experience in the pitfalls of an educational career announced: *"If I could invent anything, I'd make some glasses with open eyeballs painted on them so you could sit in class and sleep and the teacher would think you were listening."*

"What does your father do?"

"He's a congressman in Washington, D.C."

"What do you think it's like in Washington?"

"George Washington rides up and down there, watching to see that nobody chops down the trees."

"My sister just had a baby, but they didn't tell me whether it's a boy or a girl, so I don't know whether I'm an aunt or an uncle."

"How do you wake up your brother in the morning?"

"I just open the door and put the cat in his room."

"How does that wake him up?"

"He sleeps with the dog."

A four-year-old boy tells me his favorite story:

"Wittle Wed Widing Hood."

"What did you learn from that story?"

"Not to talk to stwange woofs."

The whole wonder and delight of childhood can be captured by a statement that a darling little girl made to me one morning.

"Have you ever been in love?"

"No," she replied, *"but I've been in* **like**."

There are times when a child will express an idea of real wisdom in a beautifully apt way. I'll never forget six-year-old Kathy's definition of a good friend:

"It's somebody who remembers your birthday, even when you forget hers."

CREATIVE ENCOUNTER #2........................A Quilt of Memorabilia

"But what can we say of the sweet, trusting innocence of childhood . . . its shy charm . . . its bright, quicksilver beauty . . . the dreaming wonder in a child's eyes?"

Journey back in time in your memory and imagination, and see yourself as a very young child again. Recapture those precious moments, and write your special memories in the appropriate places in the quilt below. Keep this page as a timely treasure.

MY FAVORITE NURSERY RHYME

MY FRIENDS

MY TOYS

MY SPECIAL BIRTHDAY PARTY

MY PETS

MY FAVORITE BEDTIME STORY

MY FAVORITE GAMES

MY FAVORITE SONGS

A SPECIAL MEMORY

"October 4 was a Saturday night. The young girl was at home in her Hollywood apartment fixing food for a friend's visit. Her parents had set her up in the apartment; she was old enough but getting lonely.

"Then her twenty-four-year-old brother got a panicked phone call. She was incoherent. She said she was losing her mind. He tried to talk to her, to calm her down, and he set out as fast as he could to get to her, to help her.

"He didn't get there in time. She jumped out of the kitchen window of her sixth-floor apartment and was dead.

"It was over very suddenly. A young life, full of promise . . . a bright career ahead . . . part of a loving family. Excitement and energy and spirit and talent and so much to live for. So much to give to other people, to make them happy. All of it ended very suddenly.

"It was only one of many dreams that died in 1969, but for me it was the only thing that mattered. She was my daughter, Diane."

Diane's tragedy is that perhaps only one adventure with LSD came back to haunt her and take her life. No measurable amount of any drug was found in her system after her death. Art can only speculate, from information supplied by some of her friends, that she had taken LSD in the past and had experienced a flash or recurring bad trip identified with hallucinogen. She was by no means a regular user.

In one shattering moment their lives were changed. Art's family came together even more closely. Their love for each other was multiplied and expressed as never before. Art dedicated his life to preventing his tragedy from happening to other families across the nation.

The news of Diane's death stunned the nation. It was staggering for Art to be jolted out of his personal anguish by the cards and letters from hundreds of men and women who understood his grief, because the same kind of thing was happening in their towns or to their families. His loss, far from being an event that ruined his effectiveness, drove him to become even more effective in helping others. Art became an internationally known spokesman for drug abuse prevention. He comforted agonized parents whose children had died from drug overdoses. The very thing that Art thought had emptied him—Diane's death—filled him with new vigor for concerted, meaningful action.

Because many people are aware of Diane's story, Art often becomes a lightning rod for those with similar problems. He tells them the two-step process he's found to work. Decide to push worry and guilt away. Get involved in helping others.

The fragrance of pain is compassion. Art's life exemplifies this quality. Art worked through the pain and anger of a broken dream, picked up the pieces of his broken heart, and pursued a new dream to mend broken hearts. The thorns of that "crushed rose" experience caused Art's heart to bleed. Yet he held on to that crushed rose and spread its fragrance to multitudes.

Sometimes you may not understand why you have to go through painful situations. Yet, it is a comfort to know that these experiences, when you need comfort, can teach you how to comfort. Thus, you can truly show compassion to others. If you had been free of pain, your heart might never have been tenderized enough to give comfort.

Let compassion be the whisper of your heart. Develop your capacity to perceive what others are going through. Draw near to encourage, to soothe, to comfort. Offer the gentle, warm fragrance of compassion to another who is chilled by adversity.

Is adversity plaguing you? Look at the pain through the eyes of a flower whose beauty has been marred. Listen to the heartbeat of a flower that's been carelessly crushed. Tenderly hold the flower and smell the lovely fragrance. When the winds of adversity blow, let the fragrance of pain—compassion—spread for miles.

CREATIVE ENCOUNTER #4 . . . . .A Mixture of Qualities

"Persistence is the quality that counts. And it's true enough: to achieve any significant degree of success or recognition in life, a person has to keep plugging away in the face of disappointments and failures and apparently endless obstacles."

Perseverance is a main ingredient in the mixture of admirable qualities. What are qualities that you admire in Art and other people (patience, humility, courage)?

Make up a creative mixture of these admirable qualities. Describe each quality by mixing sounds, objects, animals, or some form of nature. Mix raindrops with the fragrance of a crushed rose, and you have compassion.

Mix a ray of sunshine with a stream in a desert, and you have joy.

Mix a bubbling brook with the sounds of a marching band, and you have enthusiasm.

Mix a feather with a breeze, and you have gentleness.

Mix _____

Mix _____

Mix _____

Mix _____

Mix _____

Mix _____

Mix _____

Imagine blending these mixtures to create a delightful aroma, a glowing array of colors, and melodious sounds of music. Stir these qualities carefully as they blossom within you. The aroma, colors, and sounds of these fine qualities in you will blend together and make your life an influence on others near and far.

Draw several of your descriptive mixtures of qualities in an illustration. After completion, share your drawings. Try to find the mixtures and representations of the qualities in one another's drawings.

". . . But you know, even though picnics are a lot of fun, when you're out there in the woods, there are a few things you shouldn't do. You can't step into a river without knowing how deep it is, or you might drown. And you can't just walk up to any animal, because it might bite you. If you see a big bear, you're going to be sensible enough to duck behind a tree. Some of the plants may be poison oak and ivy, so you have to stay away from those.

"Well, just as you have to be careful on a picnic so that you won't spoil your fun, you also have to be careful about certain special things in life. For example, a match is good because it helps you light the stove so you can cook food and eat; but it can be bad because if you're careless, you might burn the house down. And knives are important as tools, but they can also cut and injure you. There's something else called drugs, which are good when you're sick, but drugs can be very bad if used for the wrong reasons or in the wrong amounts . . . ."

Art was expecting an older group of students, but instead when he walked onto the stage, he found himself facing a large group of second graders. Standing in front of them, with only a few seconds before they grew quiet, he silently had to revise his speech. He "drew" a word picture and took them on a hike and picnic in the forests of their fantasies. Art recommends we paint interesting word pictures with storybooklike anecdotes and illustrations.

In *The Key to Your Child's Heart*, Gary Smalley explains how we can utilize word pictures. An emotional word picture is associating our feelings with either a real or imaginary experience. The use of emotional word pictures is useful for children as well as adults. First, we need to clearly identify what we are feeling—what's going wrong or how do we **feel** about what's happening around us? Second, once these feelings are identified, we must make up a story that illustrates these feelings. Word pictures can also be used to praise, encourage, or point out a person's potential. They can be created by using things that are common to our experience: animals, water, mountains, desert, furniture, the seasons.

Gary Smalley talks about using word pictures as a powerful tool in communication. Spoken words are often one-dimensional, but a word picture can be multidimensional. Words have incredible power to build us up or tear us down emotionally. Just like a forest fire, words can burn deeply into our hearts. Stories hold a key to our hearts that simple words do not.

Use word pictures as the key to open the door of communication. In your speeches and in your everyday conversations, try to analogize your thoughts and feelings in word pictures. Now for practice, divide into small groups and "paint" pictures with words. Use word pictures to express your feelings, encourage or praise a friend, or give a speech. Draw a picture of your word picture.

CREATIVE ENCOUNTER #6 ....The "Art" of Public Speaking

"Perhaps the most important thing to learn and remember in your attempt to banish your fright is that talking to groups can be fun."

Use the following techniques from *Public Speaking for Private People* to help develop your speaking skills. Refer to Art's book for more tips, and give a speech on a topic of your choice.

Create opportunities for speaking practice. A tape recorder is a valuable tool to evaluate your speaking efforts.

The way you start a speech can determine how well you deliver it and what kind of ultimate impression you make on your audience. Speak simply and straightforwardly from the outset.

Pick the stories that illustrate the points you want to make and put it all together in an easy-flowing pattern with no sudden transitions. Be sure you have a logical beginning, a high point somewhere in the middle, and a sincere, prompt ending. And when in doubt, keep it short.

Some nervous tension is absolutely essential to a good speech. The best kind of nervousness is a heightened sense of your powers—perhaps something akin to the anticipation an Olympic athlete feels as he gets ready to run a big race.

Before getting up to speak, get away for a few minutes to be by yourself to visualize the audience as a warm, friendly, responsive group. Focus on getting outside yourself when you face your listeners. Keep your eyes and your attention always moving outward, rather than inward. Get more interested and absorbed in your audience than in yourself.

CREATIVE ENCOUNTER #7 ....Butterflies in Formation

"So no matter how jittery you feel now—how hopelessly nervous you may get before a talk—you can master that anxiety and deliver a good speech. Don't give up until those butterflies inside your stomach are flying in perfect formation!"

Here are four speaking games that Art has found to be a lot of fun. These games give you the speech-making skills of becoming articulate, thinking quickly on your feet, and developing your imagination.

The Storyteller

Think of some outlandish topics for stories, such as "Why Coconuts Have Hair." Then have everybody gather around in a circle. Throw out one of these topics to each person in turn and ask him to make up a story about it. None of the topics should be disclosed in advance so that everybody has to speak entirely off-the-cuff, without any prior preparation.

Continue the Story

Throw out a topic like "My Day on the Amazon River," and start to tell a story. Then look over at a friend and say, "You continue the story!" It will be up to him to come up with a solution and carry the story on to another difficult problem where another person will pick it up.

The Interview Game

Come up with several provocative topics, such as, "You're a big game hunter who has just returned with the biggest elephant tusks in history." Then announce a topic, point to someone, and start asking questions. Set a time limit on the interview, such as three minutes. The idea is to keep pouring the questions on, one after the other, with as little hesitation between each as possible.

The Sixty-Second Speech

The main idea is to assign a person at the back of the room to hold a watch with a second hand and keep track of how long different people in the group talk. Each talker should try to time his conversation so that he stops as close to the sixty-second mark as he can. You can assign amusing topics or the person can make up a story as he goes along. Also, it's often fun to arrange the sixty-second test in the form of an interview, with a leader asking the questions and the person who is supposed to be stopping the clock doing the answering.

INDEPENDENT PROJECTS—LINKLETTER

1. Art has interviewed hundreds of children. Now it's your turn to interview Art on your own *House Party* program. Produce a television show where children interview adults. Decide who will take the roles of emcee, producer, Art, Walt Disney, and other guest stars. For your next production, interview children of various ages.

2. *"Fine-tuning your sense of humor—learning to laugh at yourself at unpleasant situations that confront you—is one of the best techniques for turning a negative incident into something more positive."* Dream up zany stunts and pranks for people to perform on your own *People Are Funny* program.

3. *"The key to self-confidence and also to success and happiness in life is to find out what you really love to do, and then do it!"* People who love their work don't have to escape from their work; they escape **into** it. Art suggests this exercise to determine your own main interests in life. Take a pencil and divide a sheet of paper into two columns. Imagine yourself at the age of seventy looking back over your life. Jot down in the first column those things that you feel would have given you the greatest sense of satisfaction. Now focus on the present. Write down the work or pastimes that appeal to you most in the second column on your paper. Compare your two lists. Discuss your interests with adults who can guide you in choosing work you would enjoy.

4. Refer to *Linkletter Down Under* and become a pioneer with Art. Make a diorama and write a diary about your ventures in settling an unexplored mini empire in Australia.

RESOURCE BOOKS—LINKLETTER

Linkletter, Art. *A Child's Garden of Misinformation.* New York: Bernard Geis Associates, 1965.

_____. *Drugs at My Door Step.* Waco, Texas: Word Books, Inc., 1973.

_____. *Kids Say the Darndest Things!* Englewood Cliffs, New Jersey: Prentice-Hall, Inc., 1957.

_____. *Kids Still Say the Darndest Things!* New York: Bernard Geis Associates, 1961.

_____. *Kids Sure Rite Funny!* New York: Bernard Geis Associates, 1962.

_____. *Linkletter Down Under.* Englewood Cliffs, New Jersey: Prentice-Hall, Inc., 1968.

_____. *People Are Funny.* Garden City, New York: Doubleday & Co., Inc., 1947.

_____. *Public Speaking for Private People.* New York: The Dobbs-Merrill Co., Inc., 1980.

_____. *The Secret World of Kids.* New York: Bernard Geis Associates, 1959.

_____. *Yes, You Can!* New York: Simon and Schuster, 1979.

Linkletter, Art, and George Bishop. *Hobo on the Way to Heaven.* Elgin, Illinois: David C. Cook Publishing Co., 1980.

_____. *I Didn't Do It Alone.* Ottawa, Illinois: Caroline House Publishers, Inc., 1980.

WALK FROM BULIMIA TO HOPE

CYNTHIA ROWLAND McCLURE

"Two weeks after returning home to Oklahoma City from Oregon, I told my story to reporters. It hit the front page of the Sunday Daily Oklahoman. My phone nearly rang off the hook. Within two weeks God enabled me to help over 100 women and families. I asked Him to guide me in my new career of sharing my story in person and writing this book in order to help other women who are dying from bulimia and anorexia.

"I resigned from the TV station and started making speeches in Arkansas and Texas. In the three months following my hospitalization, I talked to over 300 desperate people, and where I spoke formed support groups for bulimics. I have also discussed communication between teens and their parents. My life is dedicated to reaching out and telling those who live with the monster bulimia that there is hope.

Cynthia Rowland McClure

BIOGRAPHICAL SKETCH

To her parents Cynthia Joye was like a miniature adult when she was growing up—the perfect child. At age four she accidentally fell into a pan of boiling water that was bubbling in a vaporizor. The scars from the severe burns made her feel inferior like damaged freight. Her father was a minister and college president in the limelight and away from home a lot, for he was responsible for so many people and jobs. Cynthia and her brother felt rejected and hurt from a lack of attention from their father.

At age fifteen, the youngest contestant in a field of fifty finalists, Cynthia was selected "Miss Teenage Christian U.S.A." This honor allowed her to travel across America and Europe speaking and writing in behalf of *Teenage Christian Magazine.* When she was a high school senior, she started binging. It was an upsetting year for her, because she moved from her childhood home, Portland, Oregon, to Oklahoma City. She started overeating for comfort and gained about ten pounds that year. Her dad offered her $300 if she would lose it for college. A girlfriend told her a way to lose weight fast. Cynthia started her new diet, and after a year her secret addiction took over. She kept thinking that if she could only be thin, her parents and other people would love and accept her.

In 1976 she received a B.A. degree in mass communications at Central State University in Edmond, Oklahoma. Since the age of 21, Cynthia was involved with every aspect of television journalism from anchoring to reporting. She covered prestigious statewide events. She interviewed people like First Lady Nancy Reagan, Mother Teresa, Barry Manilow, and former President Gerald Ford. In 1980 she covered the New York Democratic Convention. She won a 1980 Associated Press Award for outstanding documentary production. Cynthia was also named outstanding young career woman in Arkansas that same year.

In April, 1983, Cynthia's television career was abruptly interrupted by bulimia that she had suffered with for twelve years. She was eating up to 20,000 calories a day without gaining weight. When she checked into the Minirth-Meier Clinic in Richardson, a Dallas suburb, she found an expert team of therapists who helped her battle and overcome the monster. She was near death due to an electrolyte imbalance. After three months of hospitalization, she resigned her journalism career to go public in the interest of aiding others suffering from this affliction. She wrote her story, a book called *The Monster Within.* Since then she has had a battle with cancer. Cynthia is happily married and heads and speaks for the Bulimia Foundation of America.

CREATIVE ENCOUNTER #1 ....A Television Journalist

Both anorexia nervosa and bulimia are characterized by a compulsive urge to control weight. Anorexia nervosa is self-induced starvation resulting in extreme weight loss. *Anorexia* means a lack of appetite for food; *nervosa* means having to do with the nerves. Bulimia, which means an abnormal hunger, is generally characterized by an eating binge that the victim deals with by means of self-induced purge. Both eating disorders are rooted in psychological causes but can often result in serious medical complications as well.

In *The Monster Within* the staff at the Minirth-Meier Clinic states that it is important to notice that bulimia is a psychiatric eating disorder that is different from overeating or heavy snacking. It is a disease marked by compulsive, uncontrollable binging and purging, accompanied by depression and, in many instances, other psychological disorders. These disorders present serious threats to one's health and ultimately to life itself. Persons with these disorders have an obsession with food and calories and a morbid fear of gaining weight.

The victims tend to be young, healthy, attractive females from fairly affluent and successful families. These disorders do occur occasionally in males, but much less often. Based on the observations at the Minirth-Meier Clinic, the patients have a tendency to be very sensitive to society's emphasis on slimness, good looks, and popularity. They strive for good grades in school and excellent performance in the arts. They tend to be perfectionists and have low self-esteem. Unresolved childhood conflicts are major factors in the eating disorders. These diseases can be treated. Cynthia's primary recommendation is that the victims and their families need to seek help from professionals who are trained in the area of eating disorders. She also suggests that if you know of someone who has an eating disorder, encourage him/her to get help.

Here are guidelines from *Walking a Thinline* that offer counsel to people who want to help a person struggling with an eating disorder. "Don't get into power struggles over food. Don't offer pat answers. Don't impose guilt. Don't blame yourself. Lovingly confront an anorexic or bulimic with her symptoms. Get professional help for family members under legal age. Get support for yourself. Find out as much as you can about eating disorders. Require the eating disordered to take responsibility for her actions. Talk openly and honestly about your feelings. Be honest with an anorexic or bulimic about her appearance. Talk about issues other than food. Listen. Show love and affection. Hang in there!"

Cynthia was an award-winning television journalist. Research the causes and treatment of obesity and/or other eating disorders and other problems or topics of interest, such as nutrition, eating habits, or physical fitness. Find other people, such as Cherry Boone O'Neill, who overcame anorexia nervosa. Set up a TV studio in your classroom. Become a television journalist and present a documentary of your research to the class. Offer hope and help to encourage people to overcome that particular problem.

CREATIVE ENCOUNTER #2 ....Root of the Problem

Mike Moore, Cynthia's therapist, said that Cynthia's monster was really that little girl inside her saying, *"Stay away from me, I'm no good, I'm damaged freight."* When she was burned and scarred as a four-year-old little girl, she then decided she was damaged freight. That little girl came to haunt Cynthia all those years whispering, *"Go ahead and destroy yourself."* It was time for Cynthia to forgive the past and start connecting with the future.

Cynthia's problem was bulimia. Some of the symptoms of her problem were a perfectionistic attitude, compulsive eating, depression, low self-image, suicidal tendencies, and the other symptoms that go along with bulimia. The root of the problem, her childhood conflicts, was discovered with professional help. This may be rather simplified, because Cynthia went through a long process with therapists.

Choose a problem you have personally faced or that someone else has faced. Analyze the problem, symptoms, and causes of the problem the best you can. Analyzing the problem can help you to face it and try to find the root causes to overcome the problem. After you face, analyze and work on solutions to your problems, look for new growth and strengthening. Your life will become like a tree firmly planted by streams of water.

Write the problem in the nest on top of the tree. Write the symptoms on the branches. Try to get to the bottom line of the problem and write the causes of the problem in the roots of the tree.

CREATIVE ENCOUNTER #3 .... Dependence on People

"How could anyone know my needs if I didn't tell them? It was acceptable to tell people, and if the first person rejected me, I could go to the next and the next until I got what I needed. All my life I'd had needs, but I was never taught to acknowledge them. I never wanted to bother anyone. I was dying inside all those years because I was determined to do everything by myself. But no longer. From now on I would acknowledge my dependence on other people."

Learn from Cynthia's valuable lesson and tell others what you are feeling and that you need them. Cynthia produced a successful heartwarming TV show on people who give, called *Gifts of the Heart*. One man planted a garden for the elderly. He once was bitter about life because he had a heart attack and had to quit the job he loved, but he found that by helping people he became happy. What tasks are easier when others help carry the load?

Draw an illustration that shows the importance of dependence on people. Draw a garden. Plan what you want to plant and how you will take care of the garden. Divide the various jobs to help share the responsibilities of taking care of a garden. Make up a motto, such as the following: The load is lightened when it is shared.

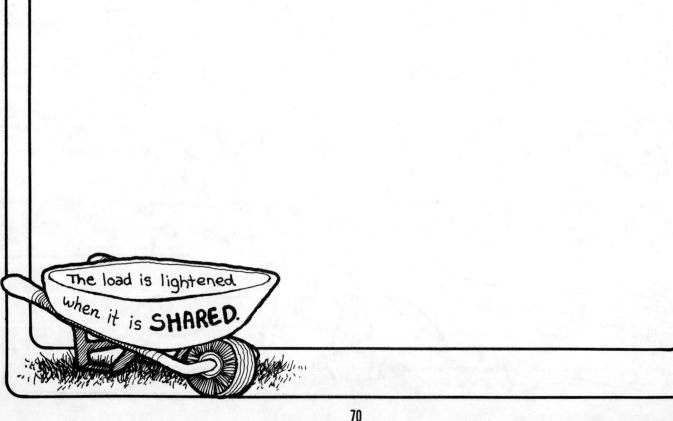

The load is lightened when it is SHARED.

CREATIVE ENCOUNTER #4 . . . . A New Menu

After Cynthia had consumed perhaps six candy bars, two pizzas, a gallon of ice cream, and more candy, and had taken sixty pink pills, she went home and tried to cry. She felt so alone. She lived only to destroy herself.

Mike Moore, her therapist, gave her this advice. *"You have to think before you eat. When you get the urge to binge and purge, it means you need people. You have to start on people binges, Cynthia. You need people."*

While Cynthia was getting ready to leave the hospital, her friend came in with a big poster that said, "I'm a People Binger." Everyone on the ward had signed it. Cynthia's life changed, when she decided to binge on people rather than food. She discovered she had a gift to perceive what others are going through. With that gift she is helping other bulimics.

Cynthia's old menu was filled with huge amounts of food that were destroying her. Make up a new menu that shows the need to reach out to people and enjoy life. For example, the new menu can include a salad of silly laughter, a filet of fun time with a friend, and a drink of fresh air while watching the sunset.

INDEPENDENT PROJECTS—McCLURE

1. Cynthia was given an assignment to write a paper entitled "What I Need from People." She said she needed acceptance, openness, love, hugs, encouragement, honesty, faithfulness, help in growing, counsel, and help in overcoming her loneliness. Write a paper with this title and express your needs.
2. In Cynthia's TV show called *Gifts of the Heart*, she did about eleven profiles. One was about a man who became a clown every Saturday and went to the hospitals to entertain the sick children. Find people in your school and community that are giving to others. Interview them on video, and present your TV production to the class.
3. *"Family therapy is an opportunity for the patient and her family members together to further explore and assess their relationships, as well as to get help in understanding her problem and information as to how to support her progress."* Research the topics of therapy, psychological testing, psychiatrist, psychologist, and/or social worker.
4. Cynthia made creative projects with crafts and clay sculpturing which allowed her to nonverbally or symbolically express her feelings. Choose a feeling—anger, sadness, happiness, etc.—and express it in a creative way in an art form of your choice.

RESOURCE BOOKS—McCLURE

Bruch, Hilde. *Eating Disorders: Obesity, Anorexia Nervosa, and the Person Within*. New York: Basic Books, Inc., 1973.

_____ . *The Golden Cage: The Enigma of Anorexia Nervosa*. Cambridge: Harvard University Press, 1978.

Christian, Shanon, and Margaret Johnson. *The Very Private Matter of Anorexia Nervosa*. Grand Rapids, Michigan: Zondervan Publishing House, 1986.

Gilbert, Sara. *What Happens in Therapy*. New York: Lothrop, Lee & Shepard Books, 1982.

Kamen, Betty, and Si Kamen. *Kids Are What They Eat: What Every Parent Needs to Know About Nutrition*. New York: Arco Publishing, Inc., 1983.

Kinoy, Barbara P. *When Will We Laugh Again?: Living and Dealing with Anorexia Nervosa and Bulimia*. New York: Columbia University Press, 1984.

Landau, Elaine. *Why Are They Starving Themselves? Understanding Anorexia Nervosa and Bulimia*. New York: Julian Messner, 1983.

Levenkron, Steven. *Treating and Overcoming Anorexia Nervosa*. New York: Charles Scribner's Sons, 1982.

O'Neill, Cherry Boone. *Dear Cherry: Questions and Answers on Eating Disorders*. New York: The Continuum Publishing Co., 1985.

_____ . *Starving for Attention*. New York: The Continuum Publishing Co., 1982.

Rowland, Cynthia Joye. *The Monster Within: Overcoming Bulimia*. Grand Rapids, Michigan: Baker Book House, 1984.

Vredevelt, Pam, and Joyce Whitman. *Walking a Thinline: Anorexia and Bulimia, the Battle Can Be Won*. Portland, Oregon: Multnomah Press, 1985.

WALK FROM SELF-DEFEAT TO SELF-ESTEEM

JOSH McDOWELL

*"My own self-image began changing from negative to positive once I started building a healthy sense of acceptance. But that change was not the result of some pop psychological pep-talk I gave myself—a 'you're a winner, you're a winner' piece of jargon said ten times each morning in the mirror. No, it was a process much more profound and much more lasting. I discovered that my acceptance was grounded in **God's nature**, who He was and who I was in Him. The knowledge of **that truth is** what really changed my inner sense of worth and value. I found a direct relationship between my **faith** in God and my acceptance of myself. When I **believed** I was truly accepted, my self-concept was affected."*

BIOGRAPHICAL SKETCH

Josh grew up on a farm in Michigan with two older sisters and a brother, all old enough to be his parents; he and his brother Jim were more than twenty years younger. When Josh was eleven years old, his oldest brother sued his parents and demanded their new house. As much as Josh loved his mother, he hated his father. Despite this hatred, Josh was grateful for the sense of responsibility his father instilled in him. Although his dad drank hard, he also worked hard.

In his senior year Josh returned home late one night to find his mother crying bitterly. She could not take any more of her husband's drinking and abuse. She told Josh she wanted to wait until after his graduation, and then she wanted to die. Josh joined the Air Force. Four months later Josh was in the hospital with a head injury, when he heard his mother died.

When Josh was a student at Wheaton College, a drunk driver hit Josh's car at 45 m.p.h., causing a collision which nearly pushed Josh's car into the path of the on-coming commuter train. It almost caused Josh to have a broken neck, which would have caused him to be paralyzed had he lived. During this time, his father gave up drinking, and Josh and his father developed a new close relationship.

Josh targeted for a law degree and became a student leader. While a student at Talbot Theological Seminary, Josh began a campus ministry and joined the staff of Campus Crusade for Christ. Josh took a Latin American Crusade to Mexico City and contracted typhoid, as well as malaria. In four days he had dropped nearly twenty-five pounds. Josh debated Marxists, Communists, and Fascists. Several times his life was threatened. Radical leaders warned Josh he would not leave Mexico alive. While he was on the way back to the United States, the radicals took a teenaged girl they had picked up and threw her in front of Josh's van. Miraculously the girl was still alive. Josh was falsely accused for driving recklessly and was taken to a dirty and primitive jail. A plan was worked out to release Josh, and soon he drove back to the United States.

Films, TV specials, books, cassettes and seminars expanded Josh's outreach to millions. He is the author of twenty-six best-selling books. Josh has spoken at more than 650 universities in seventy-four countries during the last twenty years to more than seven million people. To prepare for his speeches, Josh reads some three hundred books a year. He is intense and spends approximately one and a half to two hours in preparation for each minute of every new talk he gives. He and his wife have four children and reside in Julian, California. Josh is a dynamic leader, and his energy and vitality constantly amaze those who know him.

CREATIVE ENCOUNTER #1........................**Sailing on a Bouncy Sea**

"The hard, inner structure of one's self-image, formed early in life, may be compared to the masts of a great sailing ship. The sails hoisted up the masts are the changing fabric of who you believe you are. The sails ride on the masts and turn with the wind. Your self-image ebbs and flows in daily interactions.

"When you receive positive messages from your environment, you ride a strong wind and think well of yourself. Your ship is in full sail. At still other times you toss and turn, roughed up by angry winds of criticism and accusations from others, or even from yourself. Sails get torn in life's storms."

In the sail that is basking in the sun, write positive messages that you have received, which have helped you to feel good about yourself. In the sail that is whipping in the storm, write negative messages that have caused you to doubt yourself. In the waves write some of life's storms that may cause your self-image to waver. Rate the stability of your self-image. Indicate your rating by coloring the rungs of the ladder. Color most of the rungs of the ladder if you feel you have a healthy self-image. Color a few of the rungs if overall you are struggling with your self-image.

CREATIVE ENCOUNTER #2 ....Your Mirror Image

You are entering a fun house with a maze of a hall of mirrors. Laughter fills the corridors, for it is a hilarious experience. As you stand in front of one mirror, you appear short and fat. Take a few steps, and you shoot up to be tall and thin. The mirrors reflect countless distorted reflections. Finally, at the end of the hall is the normal mirror which gives you back your true image.

The way we view ourselves depends on where we see our reflections. Looking at the wrong mirror can give a distorted perspective. The Too-Tall Mirror represents an unrealistically high standard, perfection. Below the Too-Tall Mirror write an unrealistic expectation that you are demanding of yourself. Draw an image in the mirror to show how it is unfair to compare yourself against an image of perfection that is unattainable. Below Somebody Else's Mirror name something that you may be comparing yourself to. Draw an illustration in the mirror to remind you that comparison can keep you from discovering your own uniqueness. The Distorted Mirror represents a reflection of how other people view us and sometimes hurt us with negative criticism. Write a negative message below the Distorted Mirror. Draw an illustration in the Distorted Mirror to show how it is dangerous to focus on the negative. Below the True Mirror write one goal to express how you will not allow yourself to look in the wrong mirror for your reflection, but will try to keep a balance by finding an accurate view of yourself. Draw an illustration in the True Mirror of yourself with a smile—the new you.

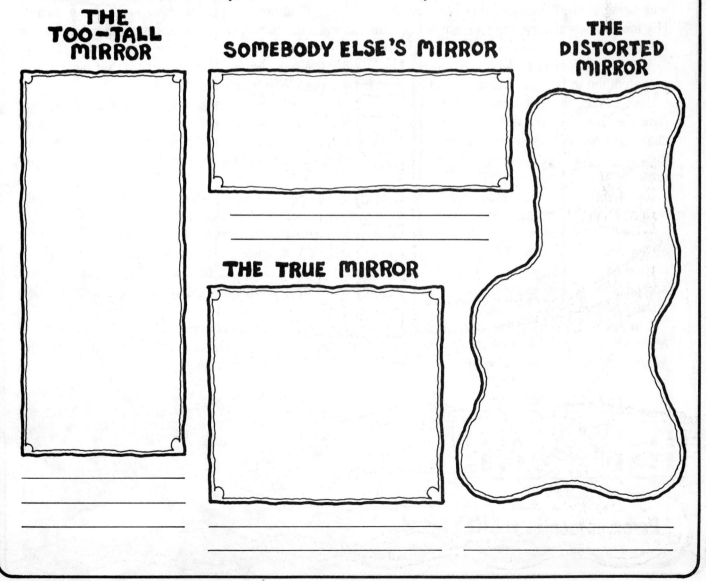

THE TOO-TALL MIRROR

SOMEBODY ELSE'S MIRROR

THE DISTORTED MIRROR

THE TRUE MIRROR

CREATIVE ENCOUNTER #3 .... Conquering Inferiority

"There was once a man whose experiences in life could well have driven him to feel inferior. At the age of seven he and his family had suffered the humiliation of being evicted from their home and having to look for a new place to live. He was forced at that age to go to work and help pay the family's bills. At age nine, his mother died, and he subsequently spent his youth feeling awkward and shy in personal relationships, particularly with girls. At twenty-three, this man went into business with a friend, but three years later the friend died leaving an enormous debt that took years to repay. At twenty-eight, he asked his long-time girlfriend to marry him, but she refused. He eventually married another woman, and the couple lost their cherished son when he was only four years old.

"This man suffered many defeats, when he ran for congressional office, U.S. Senate, and a vice-presidential nomination. Yet in the fall of 1860 this man, Abraham Lincoln, was elected sixteenth President of the United States. Though he could have succumbed to a sense of inferiority after a life filled with heartache and defeat, he persisted.

"Our task is not to avoid this feeling of inferiority, because the truth is we all experience it. Our task is rather to learn how to handle it so that it does not gain a foothold in our emotional system," states Dr. Les Carter in his book *Mind Over Emotions.*

Each setback that Abraham Lincoln encountered became his stepping-stone to success. His character was being shaped, molded, and polished through these "failures" to prepare him to lead our nation. His life and his persevering attitude is such an example to encourage us to persevere. Perseverance is the key.

What qualities are evident in Abraham Lincoln's life? What specific ways do you see that his setbacks prepared him to become President? List some of his successes after he became President.

Josh makes these statements in his speeches. *"Most of you here struggle with two fears. One, you have the fear that you will never be loved, and two, the fear that you will never be able to love."* Josh challenges you with these two questions. 1. What are you worth as a person? Not, what are the chemicals in your physical body worth, but what are **you** worth? 2. Are you happy (or excited) about who you are?

Discuss these various issues concerning self-image with your class. What is the definition of *self-image*? Describe the attributes of a person with an unhealthy self-image. Do you have confidence in your ability to deal with problems even when you experience setbacks or failures? Do you see them as learning experiences? Why is it important to make it a practice to protect another person's image, reputation, or feelings? Does your security and identity enable you to be open with people? Do you accept other people as they are and seek to understand their uniqueness? Why is it important to have an accurate view of who you are?

Charles R. Swindoll states in his book *Starting Over, "There's a philosophy of life here I'm convinced is worth one's pursuit. Here it is: The person who succeeds is not the one who holds back, fearing failure, nor the one who never fails . . . but rather the one who moves on in spite of failure."*

Perseverance is the KEY!

CREATIVE ENCOUNTER #4 .... Stepping-Stones to Success

"Talk about self-image. I was allergic to myself!

"When I entered college, my down-home grammar caught up with me. It was so poor that I was told I was a 'straight D' student. I became embarrassed to speak up in class. Then a professor told me I had two things going for me. First was the ability to put arguments and facts together to prove a point. Second was a tremendous determination and drive."

Think of setbacks that may have caused you to doubt your ability or yourself. We are going to look at these setbacks with a new perspective. Setbacks can be stepping-stones to success. Failures, difficult circumstances, and trials can be used as stepping-stones to more effective ways of helping others. Instead of looking at your setbacks as causes to feel badly about yourself, see them as stepping-stones that are leading you on the pathway to success.

Write setbacks that you have encountered on the stones. Write some things that are positive about the setbacks by the bridges. At the end of your pathway draw a symbol to represent your goal. On another sheet of paper specifically tell what you have learned from these setbacks and how you positively see them as stepping-stones.

77

"I am naturally left-handed, but as a grade school child I was forced by my teachers to change from being left-handed to being right-handed. One teacher, Mrs. Duel, stood over me with a ruler to slap my left hand if I reached out for anything with it. 'Think, Josh,' she would say. 'Use your right hand!' I came to believe that left-handedness was inferior to right-handedness, and therefore I was inferior. As a result of my feelings of inferiority and the nervousness created by such treatment, I developed a speech impediment. My poor self-image and low self-esteem were compounded by my inability to speak properly. Not only did I feel clumsy and inadequate, but now stupid as well, as I struggled to speak in front of my peers when called on in class.

"And yet, these painful memories do not compare with the devastation caused in my life by my father. To me he was the town alcoholic. My friends in high school made jokes about him. They didn't think it bothered me. I laughed on the outside, but cried on the inside. My mother wasn't just overweight. Because of a glandular condition, she was obese. As a result, I always saw myself as being fat when I wasn't."

Memories, both good and bad, form our self-image. A giant stumbling block is carrying bad memories from the past. We journey through life dragging the chains of mistakes. These real and imagined regrets hold us down and create pain. We must stop trying to rearrange yesterday. If we refuse to forget the past, we sacrifice the present and the future.

Dr. James Dobson states in his book *Preparing for Adolescence* that as young people grow up in our American society today, there are three things that they feel they **must** have in order to feel good about themselves: physical attractiveness, intelligence, and money. Human worth is not to be measured with these yardsticks. The reason we often feel unimportant and insecure is because we measure ourselves by these wrong yardsticks. When you measure yourself by someone else's yardstick, you will not come up with an accurate view of yourself. Dr. Dobson says, *"Don't listen to that little voice inside you which says, 'You're not really worthy; you're a failure; there's something wrong with you; you're different; everything will go wrong.' Don't believe it!"*

Josh states that an inadequate self-image robs us of the energy and powers of attention to relate to others because we are absorbed with our own inadequacies. Persons with an unhealthy self-image have a fearful, pessimistic view of the world and of their ability to cope with its challenges. Without self-acceptance it is hard to love or accept someone else and to accept yourself the way you are. You begin to project a person who isn't really you. To compensate for his weaknesses, Josh worked harder than everyone else at chores, studies and athletics. As a result, he excelled in studies and at sports, all the while expecting to fail in both areas.

Dr. Les Carter states that almost everything you do is a direct reflection of your self-image. He makes this analogy. Picture a wagon wheel with self-image as the hub. Your behavior and feelings are spokes extending from the hub. When your self-image is in good condition, it follows that your behaviors and feelings will be in line. Or, if your behaviors and feelings are going haywire, there is a problem at the hub, your self-image.

Use the above information about the causes and effects of an unhealthy image for class discussion. List causes of a lack of self-acceptance on the board. Then list negative effects and results of an inadequate self-image. Use this list of causes to help you be aware and face the problem of coping with a lack of self-acceptance. Use the list of negative effects to help provide the motivation to work to rise above these negative effects. Think of ways to rise above these causes and effects. The road to a better self-image may be a bumpy and difficult one, but it's important to face the causes and effects so then you are ready to begin to try to develop a new way of thinking about yourself.

"A healthy self-image shows itself in other ways, too. A stewardess was standing there saying, 'Welcome, thanks for flying with us,' while holding a dozen roses. Now I've flown close to five thousand flights (I count every one of them), but I had never seen a stewardess with her arms full of flowers.

"I said to her, 'Oh, your boyfriend bought you some flowers?'

" 'No,' she said.

" 'Well, then,' I continued, 'who did?'

" 'I did,' she said. Now that was strange.

" 'Why did you buy yourself a dozen roses?'

"She responded, 'Because I like myself.'

"Think of that. Because she liked herself she went out and bought herself a dozen roses. Maybe the time has come for you to go out and buy yourself a dozen roses."

The following are habits to develop to enhance your self-image suggested by Josh. Discuss these with your class. Write each suggestion on a card. On the other side of the card write a statement how you will specifically put a plan into action to help improve your self-image. Keep the cards in a place that you can easily refer to them.

1. Do not label yourself negatively ("I am clumsy" and so on). You tend to become the label you give yourself.
2. Behave assertively (but not aggressively) even in threatening situations, particularly when you don't feel like doing so.
3. Be as kind to yourself as you would be (or would hope to be) to any other person.
4. Do not compare yourself with others. You are a unique person.
5. Associate with friends who are positive, who delight in you and who enjoy life.
6. Start helping others by accepting them, loving them, and encouraging them.
7. Learn to laugh; look for the humor in life and experience it.
8. Have expectations of others which are realistic, taking into account each person's specific talents, gifts, abilities and potential.
9. Relax and take it easy.
10. Do what is right. When our lives reflect good character, we are a lot happier and it affects our attitude about ourselves.
11. Be positive. See how long you can go without saying something negative about another person or situation.
12. Lead others with influence and wise guidance rather than with autocratic power.

Try to live out these words of advice by Charles R. Swindoll in his book *Three Steps Forward, Two Steps Back.* *"It really boils down to what you choose to think about yourself. No one can make you feel inferior without your consent. Only you can ultimately stop the plague of self-doubt. Only you."*

1. Josh explains there are three basic emotional needs common to all people. *"These are: 1. The need to feel loved, accepted; to have a sense of belonging 2. The need to feel acceptable; to have a sense of worthiness 3. The need to feel adequate; to have a sense of competence. Picture your self-image as resembling a three-legged stool. It doesn't take much imagination to picture what happens to a person who tries to use a stool with one leg broken or too short."*
Draw an illustration of the stool and label the three legs with these three needs. Then write a personal analysis of your own needs in each of these areas. How can you help meet these needs in other people's lives?

2. Novelists go into a lot of detail describing the physical appearance, abilities, intelligence, and personal traits of the characters in their books. If someone decided to write a story about you, how would he describe you? Build your elaboration skills and write a detailed description of your friend. Ask your friend to write a description about you.

3. Write a poem entitled "Me."

4. In 1929 a University of California football player, Roy Riegels, made Rose Bowl history. In the second quarter he grabbed a Georgia Tech fumble and headed for the wrong end zone. At the half, Roy said that he couldn't face the crowd, but the coach insisted he go back in the game. Roy played harder than ever and helped bring his team to victory. Write about a time when someone believed in you and accepted you unconditionally. Interview an adult and write about a similar experience in his life.

RESOURCE BOOKS—McDOWELL

McDowell, Josh. *Building Your Self-Image.* Wheaton, Illinois: Tyndale House Publishers, Inc., 1984.

_____ . *How to Help Your Child Say "No" to Sexual Pressure.* Waco, Texas: Word Books, 1987.

_____ . *More Than a Carpenter.* Wheaton, Illinois: Tyndale House Publishers, Inc., 1977.

_____ . *The Secret of Loving.* San Bernardino, California: Here's Life Publishers, Inc., 1985.

_____ . *Teens Speak Out: What I Wish My Parents Knew About My Sexuality.* San Bernardino, California: Here's Life Publishers, Inc., 1987.

_____ . *Why Wait? What You Need to Know About the Teen Sexuality Crisis.* San Bernardino, California: Here's Life Publishers, Inc., 1987.

McDowell, Josh, and Dale Bellis. *Evidence for Joy: Unlocking the Secrets of Being Loved, Accepted and Secure.* Waco, Texas: Word Books, 1984.

McDowell, Josh, and Paul Lewis. *Givers, Takers and Other Kinds of Lovers.* Weaton, Illinois: Tyndale House Publishers, Inc., 1980.

Musser, Joe. *A Skeptic's Quest: Josh McDowell's Search for Reality.* San Bernardino, California: Here's Life Publishers, Inc., 1984.

Narramore, Bruce. *You're Someone Special.* Grand Rapids, Michigan: Zondervan Publishing House, 1978.

Wagner, Maurice E. *The Sensation of Being Somebody: Building an Adequate Self-Concept.* Grand Rapids, Michigan: Zondervan Publishing House, 1975.

Wright, H. Norman. *Improving Your Self-Image.* Eugene, Oregon: Harvest House Publishers, 1983.

WALK FROM BURNOUT TO TIME-OUT

PAUL MEIER

"Perhaps the most tragic result of workaholism is its effect on the family. I have asked many highly regarded older men what they would change if they could live their lives over. Almost without exception, they said they would have spent a little less time doing work and more time with their own children.

"One of the tragic paradoxes of burnout is that the people who tend to be the most dedicated, devoted, committed, responsible, highly motivated, better-educated, enthusiastic, promising, and energetic suffer from burnout. Why? Partially because those people are idealistic and perfectionistic. They expect too much of themselves as well as of others. Also, since they started out performing above average, others continue to expect from them those early, record-breaking results over the long haul, even though no one would expect a runner in the one-hundred-yard dash to keep up that same speed in a cross-country run."

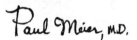

BIOGRAPHICAL SKETCH

Paul was the son of hard-working, German immigrant parents. He grew up hearing the old German motto: *Arbeit macht das Leben suss* ("work makes life sweet").

His parents rewarded him for good grades and would frown at occasional poor grades. They also attended all the elementary school open houses to see and praise the good work their children had done. It was this background that influenced Paul to continue his education for twenty-five years (thirteen before high school graduation, counting kindergarten, and twelve after).

Having grown up with an overdose of the work ethic, he was an honor student who was somewhat overzealous. One year in college, Paul carried thirty-nine hours in two semesters, played two sports, worked nights as a private nurse, was the president of two campus organizations, read a book a week in addition to his studies, did charitable work on weekends, got engaged to be married, and won an award at the end of that school year for having achieved a straight-A record.

Paul was proud of being a workaholic, when he was a premed major in college, single, and twenty years old. It enabled him to finish graduate school, medical school, and a residency in psychiatry in the decade that followed. But at the age of thirty, he was teaching counseling courses full-time. The problem was that he also found himself carrying on a part-time psychiatric practice in Milwaukee, taking courses himself, counseling people evenings in his home, and participating in seminars nearly every weekend. By that time he had three children under the age of four. Feeling overwhelmed at times, he made a major decision to rearrange his priorities.

Paul is a psychiatrist and Executive Vice-President of the Minirth-Meier Clinic, a medical and counseling center, in Richardson, a suburb of Dallas. Their daily radio program, entitled, "Minirth-Meier Clinic," is broadcast nationally through the Moody Broadcasting Network. Paul is also author or coauthor of more than twenty books and has degrees in medicine, psychiatry, and theology. He is married and the father of four children.

Paul is spending much more time with his four children than he would have if he had not seen in his psychiatric practice so many bad results of father absence. Paul believes the quantity of time spent with children is just as important as the quality of time.

CREATIVE ENCOUNTER #1 .... Tune Out to Tune In

"One of the most important factors is, of course, to keep open lines of communication between parent and child."

Our endeavor is to tune out the distractions and tune in to solely listen to the other person. How well are you tuning out to tune in?

Go beyond the horizon of just hearing, and sense the heartbeat of the other person. Many are crying on the inside. Can you hear it? Just as a mother awakens when she hears her baby whimper, our antenna needs to be in tune with other people.

Try to see listening as a three-dimensional process. Listen with your ears, eyes, and heart. Measure your listening ability. What is the width, height, and depth of your listening ability?

Be quick to listen, but listen slowly. The speed of our lives breaks down communication. Often we are so preoccupied with the fast pace, we listen halfheartedly. Not seeking advice, sometimes a person just wants a friendly, sympathetic listener. Our responses will be much wiser, if we patiently absorb what the other person is saying.

Make the decision to be an active listener, rather than acting like you are listening. Listening takes self-discipline and concentration. How often do you start listening and then go off the listening track? Do you derail the listening process by letting your mind wander while the other person is talking?

Make it a habit to look directly in another person's eyes in a conversation. What are the eyes saying? What do you hear by observing the other person's facial expressions, gestures, and mannerisms?

Good listeners keep the information shared confidential. Good listeners are interested. Good listeners do not interrupt verbally or nonverbally. List other characteristics of good listeners. Specify three behaviors you will either change or begin, during this next week, to improve your listening ability.

CREATIVE ENCOUNTER #2 .... Workaholic Burnout

"Our definition of a workaholic is an individual who has a dependence on overwork, a dependence which has a noticeable disturbance on the rest of his life."

Keep your candle lit to extinguish burnout. Don't let overwork blow out your candle. Leisure, stillness, silence, and rest will help keep your candle glowing. Take time out to fight the fire of burnout. Work on overcoming workaholism.

Dr. Meier encourages workaholics to keep the good traits of workaholism and overcome the unhealthy traits. The following questions are from *How to Beat Burnout* for self-examination and discussion to reverse the emotional part of burnout.

Have you laughed several times today? What percentage of your self-talk was positive today? What amount of time this past week did you spend living in the present? Did you do something three times this week for relaxation and recreation? How often were you stuck on "Plan A," your routine schedule, this month? How much change have you experienced during the past year? Have you done something good for one person this week? Have you forgiven the last three people who offended you? How many times has envy affected you this year? Did you talk with someone three times this week about your feelings? Did you share your burdens with a friend this week? Did you do at least one specific thing this week to become closer to a relative—a parent, brother, sister, or other close relative?

CREATIVE ENCOUNTER #3 . . . . Constructive Conflict

"At times, being with my four children can be frustrating. Sometimes I am irritated by their griping and squabbling. But I have to admit, my involvement in my children's lives is by far the most profitable investment I could ever have made."

Divide into small groups. Think of a real-life situation where conflict arises in a family. Role-play a dialogue between family members and resolve the conflict. Reverse roles. After your family conference, talk about family conflicts, sibling rivalry, and discipline.

Constructive conflict can build relationships, help you grow, and deepen your love for each other. Use the following tips for conflict resolution from *How to Beat Burnout:*

Use "I" messages—"I feel," "I need," "I want"—instead of "you" statements—"you should," "you shouldn't."

Avoid attacking each other's character; explain only the specific behavior that offends.

Ask for some kind of specific change, keep the issues to the present, and avoid bringing up the past.

Listen to one another.

Don't let your emotions get out of hand.

Resist the temptation to keep track of who won past conflicts.

Ask for and give feedback to each other.

Take time to discuss feelings.

CREATIVE ENCOUNTER #4 . . . . Balance Is the Key

What is one of your greatest strengths? Have you found when something goes out of balance that your strength can turn into a weakness? You may be sensitive-perceptive to others' feelings and needs. The flip side of your sensitive nature is that at times you may get your feelings hurt easily. You may be conscientious in your work, but it could turn into a tendency toward perfectionism. The flip side of being goal-oriented could be workaholism.

Understanding that the weakness has a positive side can help you work to flip it back to that side. Dwelling on your weaknesses can weight us down and cause discouragement. We need to weigh our strengths and weaknesses and keep them in balance.

Draw a balance scale. Write down three of your greatest strengths on one side of the scale. Analyze what would be the flip side of each strength, and write your weaknesses on the other side of the scale. Which side weighs more? Are your strengths and weaknesses in balance?

What are tangible things that require balance (a bicycle, a balance beam)? Think of intangible areas in life that we need to keep in balance (being idealistic and being realistic, work and leisure).

CREATIVE ENCOUNTER #5 . . . . Time Management Skills

To overcome workaholism and to spend less pressured time with work, sharpen your time management skills. Take the time to evaluate your skills. These practical suggestions are from *How to Beat Burnout.*

1. Take inventory of your usage of time. Invest time in scheduling, making lists of things to be accomplished, and prioritizing that list. Plan ahead, allowing sufficient time for interruptions.

2. Learn to concentrate on the task at hand. Learn to distinguish between essential details and nonessentials.

3. Be able to grasp the big picture. Work at "majoring on the majors." Be sure to relate your daily tasks to overall life goals and even to "five-year goals."

4. Work at being decisive. Get all the information available and then make a decision. Avoid procrastination.

5. Learn to delegate, particularly those things that can be done effectively by other people. Don't spread yourself too thin.

CREATIVE ENCOUNTER #6 .... Impeccable Perfectionists

"Each of us talks to ourselves. The way in which we talk to ourselves has a great deal to do with how we feel. Self-talk that is negative, derogatory, or critical fosters depression. Make an effort to be more positive, kind, and forgiving in the things you say to yourself. Why not set aside a time to consider how you talk to yourself? Look for specific changes. Forgive yourself when necessary and move on from personal failures."

Perfectionists are hard on themselves. Sometimes it seems easier for perfectionists to forgive others rather than to forgive themselves. Little things, like a smudge on a paper, leaving a few minutes late, or getting an A- instead of an A really frustrate a perfectionist. However, we do need a certain degree of perfectionism but not to the breaking point of workaholism or pessimism.

Think of at least three specific times when you drove yourself toward perfectionism. Use the chart below from *The Birth Order Book* to evaluate your perfectionistic tendency. In what ways can you keep it in balance?

Catch yourself when you are striving to reach for the unattainable level of perfectionism. Remember to be kind to yourself. Seek to be real, not perfect. When you find yourself striving to be a perfectionist, try to become a pursuer of excellence.

Perfectionists	Pursuers of Excellence
reach for impossible goals	enjoy meeting high standards that are within reach
value themselves by what they do	value themselves by who they are
get depressed and give up	may experience disappointment, but keep going
are devastated by failure	learn from failure
remember mistakes and dwell on them	correct mistakes, then learn from them
can only live with being number one	are happy with being number two, if they know they have tried their hardest
hate criticism	welcome criticism
have to win to keep high self-esteem	finish second and still have a good self-image

CREATIVE ENCOUNTER #7 .... Maxi and Mini Vacations

*"**Leisure** comes from the Latin word **licere**, which means 'to be permitted.' More today than ever, we need to learn how to give ourselves permission to relax, to play, and to enjoy life,"* states Tim Hansel.

In *When I Relax I Feel Guilty*, Tim suggests taking different kinds of vacations: super-maxi, maxi, mini, midget, and minute vacations. He entitles some of his ideas for active rest back-roads vacations, cheap vacations, memory lane vacations, a wonder trip, exploration vacations, once-in-a-lifetime specials, and a vacation from complaining.

Are there minutes in a day you could convert into vacations? What about limiting your mini vacation to one tank of gas, going anywhere you can and investing yourself as much as you can? List all the places you can explore for nothing.

Brainstorm ideas for maxi and mini vacations for family fun. Relax, take an imagination vacation, and plan a vacation of your dreams. Draw a story map of your vacation.

My Son Grows Up

My hands are busy through the day,
I didn't have much time to play
The little games you asked me to.
But when you'd bring your teddy bear
And ask me please to share your fun,
I'd say: "A little later, son."
I'd tuck you in all safe at night
And hear your prayers, turn out the light,
Then tiptoe softly to the door . . .
I wish I'd stayed a minute more.
For life is short, the years rush past . . .
A little boy grows up so fast,
No longer is he at your side,
His precious secrets to confide.
The teddy bears are put away,
There are no longer games to play,
No good-night kiss, no prayers to hear . . .
That all belongs to yesteryear.
My hands, once busy,
now are still.
The days are long
and hard to fill,
I wish I could
go back and do
The little things
you asked me to.

—Author Unknown

Reprinted with permission from
Abbey Press, St. Meinrad, Indiana 47577
All rights reserved.

CREATIVE ENCOUNTER #8 ....A Page for Parents

"One main way to guarantee consistency in discipline is to use written family contracts. When the children are very young, a family contract may need revision only once every year or two. But during the teenage years, it may need revision every two or three months. A lengthy family council meeting is the best time to write up a family contract, and everyone in the family should participate in creating it. If the children are quite varied in their ages, separate contracts, or at least separate sections on the large family contract, will probably be necessary for each child.

"Ask the children for their opinions of what the rules and chores ought to be. As the children make their suggestions, the family can vote on each one, with the father having veto power, of course.

"When listing rules, chores, and consequences, it is extremely important to be very specific. The consequence should also be specific and should (as much as possible) be related to the offense. If he lives up to his part of the contract, there will be absolutely no need to nag him. If he doesn't keep his part of the bargain, the parent still won't need to nag—just automatically give him the consequence he listed on the right side of the line. If he breaks a rule, he suffers the consequence he agreed upon."

Our Family Contract

Rules and Chores	Consequences

INDEPENDENT PROJECTS—MEIER

1. *Love* is spelled t-i-m-e. What does the poem in this unit say to you? Write a poem about the gift of time as an expression of love and the importance of quality and quantitiy time spent with the family.

2. Surprise each member of your family with priceless coupons. Each coupon is a token of your love by giving your time to help. For example: This coupon entitles you to an afternoon with me to help you rake leaves. (Take a break and make the work fun. Build a fort of leaves. Have a leaf-throwing contest or a leaf fight.)

3. We can appreciate the gift of work and the joy we find in contributing to the lives of other people through our skills. Find out about your family's work heritage. Draw a family tree. Write each family member's vocation by his/her name. Include what you might like to do as your life's work. Contrast vocations of past generations to vocations available today.

4. Dr. Meier lists five factors consistently found in mentally healthy families: love, discipline, consistency, example, and a man at the head of the home. Give a speech, flavored with help and hope, on one of the following topics: sibling rivalry, children and divorce, step families, adoption, single parents, broken homes, or characteristics of workaholics or perfectionists.

5. Plan a family appreciation dinner. Create your own centerpiece. On the inside of the place cards, write personal thank-you messages. Write a poem of appreciation for your parents on a scroll. Plan the menu and help with the meal.

 ## RESOURCE BOOKS—MEIER

Coleman, William L. *What Children Need to Know When Parents Get Divorced.* Minneapolis: Bethany House Publishers, 1983.

Coyle, Neva, and Marie Chapian. *Slimming Down and Growing Up.* Minneapolis: Bethany House Publishers, 1985.

Galbraith, Judy. *The Gifted Kids Survival Guide* (for ages 11-18). Minneapolis: Free Spirit Publishing Co., 1983.

Johnson, Rex. *Communication: Key to Your Parents.* Eugene, Oregon: Harvest House Publishers, 1978.

Kehle, Mary. *In the Middle: What to Do When Your Parents Divorce.* Wheaton, Illinois: Harold Shaw Publishers, 1987.

Krementz, Jill. *How It Feels to Be Adopted.* New York: Alfred A. Knopf, 1983.

_____. *How It Feels When Parents Divorce.* New York: Alfred A. Knopf, 1984.

Kuntzleman, Charles T. *The Well Family Book.* San Bernardino, California: Here's Life Publishers, Inc., 1985.

LeShan, Eda. *Grandparents: A Special Kind of Love.* New York: Macmillan Publishing Co., 1984.

_____. *What's Going to Happen to Me? When Parents Separate or Divorce.* New York: Four Winds Press, 1978.

Minirth, Frank, Don Hawkins, Paul Meier, and Richard Flournoy. *How to Beat Burnout.* Chicago: Moody Press, 1986.

Minirth, Frank, Paul Meier, Frank Wichern, Bill Brewer, and States Skipper. *The Workaholic and His Family.* Grand Rapids, Michigan: Baker Book House, 1981.

RESOURCE BOOKS FOR PARENTS

"I would encourage you to love your children unconditionally. Give them hugs. Frequently tell your children you love them. Another way to show love for our children is to have genuine love between husbands and wives."

"Spend a lot of time listening to their feelings. When they are angry, even toward you, encourage them to verbalize that anger in a polite, tactful, and respectful way. Let them share their feelings of insecurity, warmth, and sadness. I think it's that quality communication time that gets left out for the children."

"Keep the standard within reach. If they come home with less than a perfect report card, and if they're making an adequate effort, praise them for what they did right."

Butterworth, Bill. *My Kids Are My Best Teachers: The ABC's of Parenting.* Old Tappan, New Jersey: Fleming H. Revell Co., 1986.

_____ . *Peanut Butter Families Stick Together: Family Life Can Be Smooth or Crunchy.* Old Tappan, New Jersey: Fleming H. Revell Co., 1985.

Chapin, Alice. *Bright Ideas for Creative Parents.* New York: Walker and Co., 1986.

Dobson, James C. *Love Must Be Tough: New Hope for Families in Crisis.* Waco, Texas: Word Books, 1983.

_____ . *Parenting Isn't for Cowards: Dealing Confidently with the Frustrations of Child-Rearing.* Waco, Texas: Word Books, 1987.

Frydenger, Tom, and Adrienne Frydenger. *The Blended Family.* Grand Rapids, Michigan: Chosen Books, 1984.

Getz, Gene A., and Elaine Getz. *Growing Together in Marriage.* Glendale, California: Regal Books, 1988.

Hart, Archibald D. *Children and Divorce: What to Expect, How to Help.* Waco, Texas: Word Books, 1982.

Houmes, Dan, and Paul Meier. *Growing in Step: Your Guide to Successful Stepparenting.* Richardson, Texas: Today Publishers, Inc., 1985.

Kesler, Jay, Ron Beers, and LaVonne Neff, eds. *Parents and Children.* Wheaton, Illinois: Victor Books, 1986.

Kesler, Jay, and Ronald A. Beers. *Parents and Teenagers.* Wheaton, Illinois: Victor Books, 1984.

Ketterman, Grace H. *A Circle of Love: How You Can Nurture Creative, Caring and Close-Knit Parent-Child Relationships.* Old Tappan, New Jersey: Fleming H. Revell Co., 1987.

_____ . *You and Your Child's Problems: How to Understand and Solve Them.* Old Tappan, New Jersey: Fleming H. Revell Co., 1983.

Leman, Kevin *The Birth Order Book: Why You Are the Way You Are.* Old Tappan, New Jersey: Fleming H. Revell Co., 1985.

_____ . *Making Children Mind Without Losing Yours.* Old Tappan, New Jersey: Fleming H. Revell Co., 1984.

Lewis, Paul, and Dave Toht. *Famous Fathers: Twelve Successful Men Share the Joy and Adventure of Being a Dad.* Elgin, Illinois: David C. Cook Publishing Co., 1984.

Meier, Paul, D. *Christian Child-Rearing and Personality Development.* Richardson, Texas: Today Publishers, Inc., 1977.

Meier, Paul, and Richard Meier. *Family Foundations: How to Have a Happy Home.* Grand Rapids, Michigan: Baker Book House, 1981.

Meier, Paul D., and Linda Burnett. *The Unwanted Generation: A Guide to Responsible Parenting.* Grand Rapids, Michigan: Baker Book House, 1980.

Narramore, Bruce. *Parenting with Love and Limits.* Grand Rapids, Michigan: Zondervan Publishing House, 1987.

Schock, Bernie. *Parents, Kids, and Sports: Making the Experience Positive.* Chicago: Moody Press, 1987.

Smalley, Gary. *The Key to Your Child's Heart.* Waco, Texas: Word Books, 1984.

Swindoll, Charles R. *You and Your Child.* Nashville, Tennessee: Thomas Nelson, Inc., 1977.

Webb, James T., Elizabeth A Meckstroth, and Stephanie S. Tolan. *Guiding the Gifted Child.* Columbus, Ohio: Ohio Psychology Publishing Co., 1982.

White, Joe. *How to Be a Hero to Your Teenager.* Wheaton, Illinois: Tyndale House Publishers, Inc., 1984.

White, John. *Parents in Pain: Overcoming the Hurt and Frustration of Problem Children.* Downers Grove, Illinois: InterVarsity Press, 1979.

Ziglar, Zig. *Dear Family.* Gretna, Louisiana: Pelican Publishing Co., Inc., 1984.

_____ . *Raising Positive Kids in a Negative World.* Nashville, Tennessee: Oliver Nelson Books, 1985.

WALK FROM YOUTH TO MATURITY

PAT MOORE

"I had a marvelous, maybe even a unique opportunity. At an important passage in my own life, with the help of makeup and 'antique' clothes, I was catapulted through the continuum we call the life span.

"What did I learn? I learned to cherish every moment, savor every experience, and grasp every opportunity. I learned that the presence of God is equally as real, and equally as precious, at any age. I learned that, after Him, people are the most important element in my life—that relationships are what matter most, and if they are right, we need not be overwhelmed by career and deadlines, pressures and fears, strange places and things. And I was reminded of the ultimate importance of loving and caring and sharing. It was a valuable lesson, a worthwhile journey."

Patricia A. Moore

BIOGRAPHICAL SKETCH

Even as a preschooler, Pat gravitated toward drawing and painting. Her father gave her a drawing board with paper and a tin can full of crayons, and her family soon came to regard art as "Pattie Anne's special gift." The Albright Art Museum in Buffalo, New York, had a tutorial art program for elementary school children, and Pat's mother, a schoolteacher, seized the opportunity for her precocious child. During that time Pat decided she wanted to be an artist.

In high school Pat was the one who designed and decorated the gym for the prom. She was in charge of getting the school's float ready for the St. Patrick's Day Parade. Entering several art contests, she won several awards for her work.

Rochester Institute of Technology had an art school with a nationwide reputation. In a personal interview she showed them her bulging portfolio of high school art, and she was accepted on the spot. A professor told her she had potential in industrial design and challenged her to try. Pat plunged into this major and found it matched her abilities and temperament. In 1974 she graduated with a B.F.A. (Bachelor of Fine Arts) degree, and immediately she landed a job with the prestigious firm of Raymond Loewy in New York City. Pat was the most junior member of the firm, and one of only three women designers, but she soon attracted the attention of top management with her creative ideas.

Pat wondered what it was like to be older. At the age of twenty-six Pat put on a gray wig and latex wrinkles with the help of a professional makeup artist. Her purpose was to research to supplement her studies in gerontology and industrial design with firsthand knowledge of the joys and frustrations of advanced age. Over the next three years, she went into character as a woman of eighty-five years in 116 cities in fourteen states and two Canadian provinces. She appeared on some occasions as a wealthy dowager with fine clothes and jewelry. On other occasions she was a lower-middle-class woman, and she also became one of those poor vagabonds called "bag ladies" who are seen on the streets in major cities. In Harlem she was brutally mugged.

Pat is a highly respected industrial designer. She is president of her own design firm, Moore and Associates, which serves major corporate clients from its offices in downtown New York. Pat's experiences in the character of an old woman have made her a symbol of the aging issue in America, and she has become a media personality.

CREATIVE ENCOUNTER #1 ....Seasons of Life

In the springtime of your life, you are like a curious fawn in the forest, watching, learning, playing and exploring your new world. As you blossom into the season of summer, those fun, youthful years, you enjoy soaking up the sun, but also experience the pain of sunburn with the difficulties that come in those years of growing and discovering who you are. The colorful autumn season of your life, the adult years, brings new responsibilities, storing up provision for the winter. The grandeur of the winter season, those sunset years filled with golden memories, is a time to care and share your wisdom and knowledge that were gained in your seasons of life with future generations.

Draw an illustration under each season that represents that season of life. Use scenes of nature, such as a golden sunset in the glistening snow-covered mountains for the winter years.

SPRING

SUMMER

AUTUMN

WINTER

CREATIVE ENCOUNTER #2 .... Journey into Your Future

"We never grow old emotionally. We all want to be loved, touched, held. Our bodies change, but our emotional needs do not. And some of the people who seemed to possess the same serenity as the elderly were, to my surprise, little children."

Pat managed to capture the feeling of being older. Her time machine was a makeup kit. Pat put on old spectacles, used a cane, wore splints and bandages under her clothes to stiffen her joints, and put plugs in her ears to dull her hearing. Her body was turned into a kind of prison. Yet, inside she did not change. Pat says that's how older people say they feel. Their bodies age, but inside they are really no different than when they were younger.

Role-play the following situations. Use various props, such as a cane or a hat. Change roles to gain new perspectives of what it feels like to be an older person. Pat encountered these situations in her character as an older lady.

Become an elderly person. You are standing alone in the middle of a crowd of young professionals at a gerontology conference. Gerontology books talk about the problems of social "dismissal" of the aging—that is, that they are apt to be ignored, dismissed, or overlooked as if they were part of the furniture or the wallpaper. Now you are getting a taste of it. Role-play how you will break through and communicate to these people who are there to learn more about gerontology but who seem to be ignoring you.

You, as an elderly person, are enjoying the time sitting on the bench in Central Park in New York City. The whole spring day is passing by—watching young children play, feeding the pigeons and chatting. You are sitting with three widows or widowers. Carry on a conversation with your peers. Pat says that in most of the conversations she observed, she heard older people talk proudly of children and grandchildren, express delighted amazement at the latest developments in science and technology, or share an eagerness to leave something behind for their families.

You are an elderly person walking along the beach in Florida. You notice sea gulls hovering nearby, attracted by a little boy six years of age, who is busily throwing pieces of bread into the air. The little boy asks you to collect shells with him. You have a cane, and he is concerned about your footing in the wet sand. Role-play this scene, where there are no "young" or "old," no barriers of age, but just friendship and laughter on a big beach with plenty of shells for two friends to share.

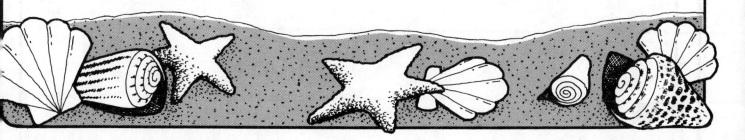

CREATIVE ENCOUNTER #3 .... The Vital Connection

"People must hear that there is nothing to fear from each other. People must know they don't have to fear their own aging, or that of people they love. There is no reason to withdraw from each other, or to give up on oneself or on each other.

*"If I could wish for any particular result from my work, it would be that people of all ages would learn that we live in a community, a society; that we are not isolated; that we are all connected, the baby, the child, the teenager, the young adult, and the senior citizen—and we are responsible **to** one another and **for** one another."*

Think of the needs of each of the above age groups. What responsibilities does each of the age groups have to the other age groups? Write an essay about these needs and responsibilities to depict how each age group needs and depends on the others.

CREATIVE ENCOUNTER #4 . . . . .An Industrial Designer

"There are so many ways in which we can improve the quality of life for older Americans by designing with their needs in mind. The answer is to design products which are equally suitable for people of all ages and levels of strength and dexterity. This approach offers us a marvelous opportunity to design a better physical environment for all Americans."

Pat studied biomechanics (the discipline that combines the needs of consumers with the design and ingenuity of products and the environment) and gerontology (the discipline that examines the social, mental, and physical aspects of people throughout their life span). Think of everyday products and appliances we use that may be difficult for older people to use.

Design a new product or improve a product with the needs of older consumers in mind. Make up a commercial for your product and act it out for your class.

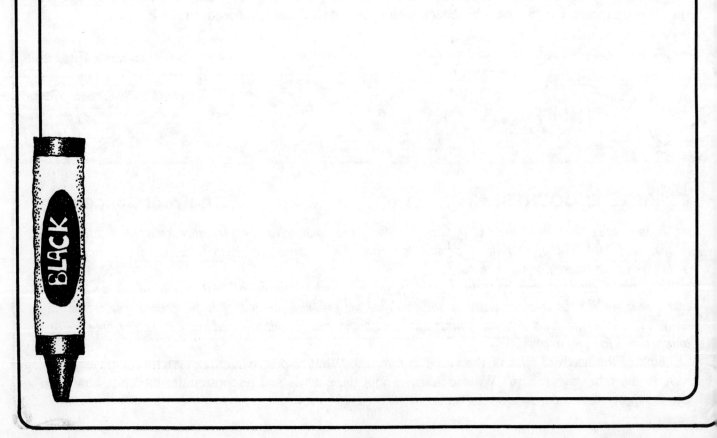

"An obvious way to combat the negative attitudes toward older people is to prevent them from developing in the first place, to teach children about aging in such a way that they never lose the natural acceptance which was displayed by my little friend on the beach in Florida."

The following are guidelines that Pat suggests to parents. There are ideas provided for you to do with your class and/or parents to go along with each guideline.

1. *"When a child notices that the elderly look and act somewhat differently from younger people, and begins to quiz you about the difference, take time to talk about it."*

Research and discuss in class the many physical changes which are often age-related, such as arthritis, failing eyesight, hearing loss, osteoporosis, arteriosclerosis, the probability of strokes, etc. Relax with any discomfort about this subject, for sometimes it is probably a simple fear of the unfamiliar.

2. *"Provide your children with as much contact as possible with older people, in as many different positive situations as possible."*

In reaching out to a wide variety of age groups, we enjoy lives which are fuller and more interesting. This diversity often means going out of one's way to create the opportunity, but it is worth the effort.

Where do you meet and talk to older people? Write an essay, entitled "Grand Person," about an older person who has had an impact on your life and who probably will influence you in the future.

3. *"Let your child see you reaching out to older people of your acquaintance."*

"Personal example is still the best teacher." Some of Pat's best memories of her father, when she was growing up, were those times when he would take his toolbox and play Mr. Fix-It for all the older people on the block.

Pat thinks that perhaps the worst thing about aging may be the overwhelming sense that everything around you is letting you know that you are not terribly important any more. On several occasions Pat went twice to the same establishments and engaged in the same transactions with the same personnel, once as the younger and once as the older character. In virtually all these comparisons, the people she encountered showed a more positive attitude toward the younger Pat.

Pat began her whole experiment with the hope that she would be better able to serve the elderly community. She was seeking to learn better how to help them, and instead, in many small interactions with older people, she could see that it was they who were helping her.

What are ways that you and your parents can become actively involved in helping older people? "Find out about that older person with whom you are casually acquainted. Does she need a ride to the grocery store every week? Would she like to baby-sit? Give her a call next time you are going to the shopping mall, and see if she might like to go or if perhaps there is something you can bring her."

Develop the art of letter writing. Write to a grandparent.

4. *"Use older citizens to help your child have a sense of 'living history.' "*

"One of the greatest gifts older people can give us is their personal recollection of the past." Invite grandparents and/or older persons to the class. Ask them to come prepared to tell stories of their past. Inquire about their family customs and activities, their school life, and what advice they would give to youth today. When you introduce that special grand person to your class, surprise him/her by telling about a memorable occasion you had together.

Past generations have given us a rich heritage in America. What do you want people to remember about you? Write about the legacy you would like to leave to future generations.

"I believe most of the elderly men and women we meet would say to us, in one way or another, 'Open your eyes and look closer at me!' Don't see the wrinkles, don't see the stereotypes; but take the time to look closely enough to see me for the person I am."

INDEPENDENT PROJECTS—MOORE

1. *"Younger people often think and talk of the disadvantages of being* **old**, *but there are advantages, too, and this is one of them. The accumulation of time can help us prioritize our lives."* Make a list of advantages and disadvantages of being young and another list for being old.
2. Dr. Albert Schweitzer was still treating patients at the age of ninety. When Winston Churchill was seventy-seven, he was reelected Prime Minister of Great Britain. At the age of eighty-one, Benjamin Franklin played a key role in the creation of the United States Constitution. Find older people throughout history who lived active, productive lives in their elderly years. Make a diorama to depict a scene of their contributions to mankind.
3. Gather the whole family for a time of listening to the older generation talk. A tape recorder or video recorder may be used to record these priceless moments. Share these stories of their past with your class.
4. Think of creative ways to express your love and appreciation for an elderly person. Make a centerpiece that looks like a small tree. Write on little pieces of paper poetic verses about your special person. Roll them up like scrolls. Tie the scrolls with colorful ribbons and put them on branches.
5. Research your family background and nationality. Try to go back as far as you can to see how your ancestry lived.

RESOURCE BOOKS—MOORE

Farber, Norma. *How Does It Feel to Be Old?* New York: E.P. Dutton, 1979.

Hayes, Helen, and Marion Glasserow Gladney. *Our Best Years.* Garden City, New York: Doubleday & Co., Inc., 1984.

Horne, Jo. *Caregiving: Helping an Aging Loved One.* Glenview, Illinois: Scott, Foresman and Co., 1985.

Kornhaber, Arthur, and Kenneth L. Woodward. *Grandparents/Grandchildren: The Vital Connection.* Garden City, New York: Doubleday & Co., 1981.

Minirth, Frank, John Reed, and Paul Meier. *Beating the Clock: A Guide to Maturing Successfully.* Richardson, Texas: Today Publishers, Inc., 1985.

Moore, Pat, and Charles Paul Conn. *Disguised.* Waco, Texas: Word Books, 1985.

Painter, Charlotte. *Gifts of Age: Portraits and Essays of 32 Remarkable Women.* San Francisco: Chronicle Books, 1985.

Raynor, Dorka. *Grandparents Around the World.* Chicago: Albert Whitman & Co., 1977.

Rosewell, Pamela. *The Five Silent Years of Corrie Ten Boom.* Grand Rapids, Michigan: Zondervan Publishing House, 1986.

Rushford, Patricia. *The Help, Hope and Cope Book for People with Aging Parents.* Old Tappan, New Jersey: Fleming H. Revell Co., 1985.

Sandler, Martin W. *The Way We Lived: A Photographic Record of Work in a Vanished America.* Boston: Little, Brown and Co., 1977.

Silverstein, Alvin, Virginia Silverstein, and Glenn Silverstein. *Aging.* New York: Franklin Watts, 1979.

WALK FROM PRISON TO FREEDOM

HAROLD MORRIS

"What does it take to be broken? I'd survived prison violence with numerous wounds, culminating in thirty-nine stitches in the head. I'd survived prison punishment and the taunting of guards. I'd survived the loneliness—five years without receiving a letter or a visit because I was too ashamed to let my family know where I was. But the absolute hopelessness is what finally broke me. After six months on death row, I simply gave up.

"During the past six years I have spoken in more than 500 high schools and junior high schools. I discuss alcohol and drugs, how to resist negative peer pressure, self-esteem, and what wrong associations can do to one's life. I stress the importance of developing a good attitude, accepting discipline at home and at school, loving and understanding one's parents. I let young people know that I love them and that Jesus died for them. I warn them of the danger of making even a little compromise, such as cheating on a test or smoking cigarettes."

Harold Morris

BIOGRAPHICAL SKETCH

Harold's mother managed to meet the needs of eleven children, helped with the chores on the farm, and worked outside the home. The discipline Harold's father administered was both swift and harsh with the abusive message, "You're no good! You'll never amount to anything."

During his senior year Harold served as captain of the basketball, baseball, and football teams at Winyah High in Georgetown, South Carolina. He was recognized as the best athlete in the school. As much as Harold wanted to further his athletic career, his scholastic record worked against him, and he had no choice but to reject the offers of athletic scholarships.

Easily swayed by peer pressure, he submitted to the standards of the older crowd to gain acceptance. Harold had a respectable job with an insurance company, a new Cadillac, and the freedom he thought he wanted. He had never been in trouble with the police, not even a ticket for parking or speeding, and he'd never seen an ex-convict. But that soon changed. On September 18, 1968, his friends, Jack and Danny, shot a man at a supermarket in Atlanta, Georgia. They jumped into Harold's car and he drove them to safety. Later his friends betrayed Harold and testified against him in court to cover for their misdeed. Falsely charged with armed robbery and murder, 29-year-old Harold faced two life sentences.

Of the 3200 men at Georgia State Penitentiary, Harold had been chosen to speak in area high schools, informing young people about alcohol, drugs, and prison life. He was chosen to head the athletic department in prison. His family and friends worked hard to help Harold become a free man. On March 1, 1978, a letter arrived from the State Board of Prison and Parole to release Harold under parole supervision. In 1981 the crime against Harold was erased, his rights as a citizen of the United States were restored, and he was no longer under probation.

Of all the killers Harold met in prison, he was totally unprepared for the one he encountered during 1984—cancer. Harold resides near Daytona Beach, Florida. A book and film about his life, both entitled *Twice Pardoned*, have been produced and released by Focus on the Family. Harold, ex-convict #62345, warns young people to avoid the snares that nearly destroyed his life. He talks about the perilous effects of peer pressure and how little mistakes can have big consequences.

CREATIVE ENCOUNTER #1 ....An Amazing Maze

Some days life amazes; other days it mazes us. In that maze we face and make decisions every day that affect our lives and the people around us.

Follow this maze. Try several of the alternate routes to discover where the paths of the various choices lead.

CREATIVE ENCOUNTER #2........................**Decision-Making Skills**

Decisions . . . Decisions. Some decisions have obvious answers—a definite yes or no. In other decisions there may be several good alternatives.

Ticktock. Ticktock. Like the pendulum on a grandfather's clock, you go back and forth wondering which way to choose. Decisions shape what happens in your life in the sands of time.

Use the following method to help you make a decision. Write the problem, the alternative solutions to the problem, the positive and negative aspects of each alternative, and your final decision.

Make it a habit throughout your life to write down the pros and cons when you are having difficulty making a decision. Weigh the consequences carefully, for your choices will shape your own footprints in the sands of time.

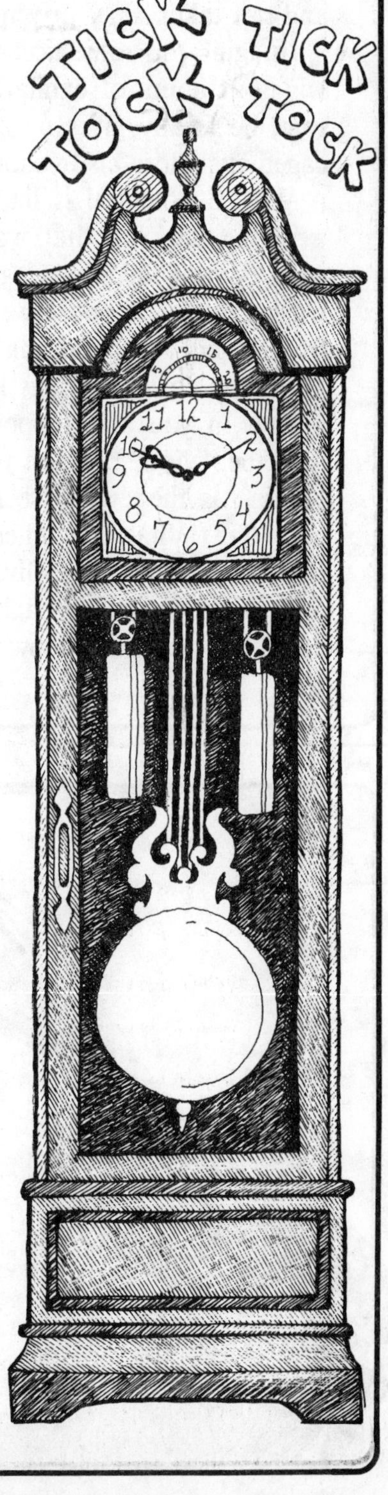

Problem: _____

_____

Alternative #1: _____

_____

Pros	Cons
1. _____	1. _____
_____	_____
2. _____	2. _____
_____	_____
3. _____	3. _____
_____	_____

Alternative #2: _____

_____

Pros	Cons
1. _____	1. _____
_____	_____
2. _____	2. _____
_____	_____
3. _____	3. _____
_____	_____

Decision: _____

_____

"One of the saddest experiences of prison is seeing wasted potential. Doctors, lawyers, athletes, and ministers are joined with common murderers, robbers, and rapists to share the wreckage of life."

Close your eyes. As your teacher reads this guided fantasy, visualize yourself watching an eagle's flight.

High in the sky, the eagle soars like a living glider, riding the wind currents, tipping, tilting, exploring illimitable ranges of the world. With a few strokes of those wings, he mounts swiftly upward, thousands of feet. Folding his wings back, he shoots toward the earth with breathtaking speed. Rising again in the sky until almost out of sight, he swoops and dips in his aerial acrobatics. Midway in his downward flight, he suddenly turns, doing an aerial somersault.

The eagle takes great joy in his flight. This keen-eyed, wide-winged creature is an independent thinker and risk taker. He is driven with this inner surge to search, to discover, to learn.

Imagine this majestic eagle captured to be imprisoned in a cage. The freedom to use his huge, strong wings in hours of exhilarating flight is relinquished. After repeated attempts to spread his wings and soar, he finally gives up such protests and sits quietly on his perch. What a sad sight it is to see this caged eagle lose his freedom and any real interest in life.

Wasted potential is like an eagle in a cage. Next time you are entertaining the thought of making a wrong decision that would result in painful consequences, envision the sad sight of an eagle in a cage. Wrong decisions can cause you to be imprisoned in a "cage" of heartache, guilt, regret, and wasted years. If you have already made those choices and are in that cage, there is hope. Seek help from others and break that lock to find new freedom to start over and try again.

Mount up your wings like eagles. Wise decisions can lead you to soar to new heights. People who believe in you and support you are like wind beneath your wings. You can fly higher than an eagle with the "wind" beneath your wings.

Who is the "wind" beneath your wings? Compare the sad sight of an eagle in a cage to wasted potential. What are different "cages" or "prisons" in life? (For example, the prison of being locked into drug addiction.) Give examples of wrong choices that lead to wasted potential like an eagle in a cage. If you're an eagle at heart, are you sitting on that perch? Do you feel out of place in that cage? Do you realize how much you are needed to soar and explore?

"Clearly it all began in high school by drinking alcohol and running with the wrong crowd. Drugs came later, and the wrong crowd became desperados whose false testimony sealed my conviction. One who crawls with animals catches fleas. So it was in my life."

It is so important to know where you stand. Know yourself. You need to have your decision already made to say no beforehand. Otherwise, when you are in a situation, it may look like fun, but in reality the consequences of your choice to give in could be devastating. If it's something that is especially difficult for you to say no to, you need to go a step further. When you unexpectedly find yourself in a luring situation, you will need to quickly leave the scene or avoid that situation altogether.

You are invited to a party. Your friends are going, and your parents have given you permission to go. You have heard rumors that someone is planning to sneak drugs to the party. You enjoy being with your friends, and you don't like to miss a good time.

You have several choices. Be open with your parents or another adult and tell them about the rumors. You know they would stand by you to protect you and help you to be accountable to make the right decision. You can decide on your own not to go, or you can go to the party. You are knowledgeable about how harmful drugs are, because you have studied them in science class. You have taken a stand. You refuse to take drugs. Yet there is a question in your mind. *"If I put myself in that situation, can I handle my friends pressuring me to take the drugs?"* Should you go and take the risk? If you go with the intention of talking your friends out of taking drugs, will you yourself succumb? If you know of students who are regularly using or trafficking in drugs, do you think you have a responsibility to somehow find help for them? Can you say no under pressure?

Think of other alternatives to handle this problem. Role-play the above situation with your friends. Take the position of saying no to a friend who is pressuring you to go to the party. Reverse roles.

*"Pride kept me from calling my precious mother during the loneliest years of my life, adding to the unspeakable pain I was already facing. When I looked into my mother's face, I finally understood how much she had suffered because of my suffering. I realized that **her** prison term ended with mine."*

The next time you are thinking about making a wrong choice, think of people who care for you. Stop and take a few moments to think how they will be hurt and the painful consequences of that choice.

Be accountable to these people, and tell them about your fears, feelings, and frustrations. Often people fall, when they are not accountable to others. Why do you think it is important to be accountable to others?

Make a chart with the following list: alcohol, drugs, suicide, and television addiction. Research and write down a few facts about each topic in a column. In another column write down the consequences when each topic is misused or abused. In the last column write your views and where you stand concerning each issue. Discuss what you have found with your parents, your school counselor, or other adults, who will uphold you and help you stay accountable.

These were the words spoken by Harold to a thirteen-year-old seventh grader contemplating suicide. Her letters to Harold indicate she is doing well, but her story wrenched his heart.

"Your whole life is ahead of you. You can be anything you want to be. These are important years of your life. You've got to make something of them. You have every reason in the world to live. Promise me you'll call before you try to take your life!"

INDEPENDENT PROJECTS—MORRIS

1. Produce a television documentary about how to make television a tool instead of being its servant. Offer practical suggestions for families to keep television viewing in balance. Make a comparison between reading and television viewing. How can a television program be used as a springboard for family discussion? What effects do commercials have upon people? How do you think television affects people who continue watching extreme violence night after night? In what ways can television with its tremendous impact be used positively as a tool for the viewer? What new information, ideas, and perspectives have you learned from television viewing?

2. If you have been affected by alcoholism in a family member or close friend, seek help from Alateen, part of the Al-Anon Family Groups. Write a paper answering these questions. What is alcoholism? What are symptoms of alcoholism? Why is alcoholism called a family disease? What effects does an alcoholic parent have upon his/her children? What hope and help are offered for these families?

3. The author of *Fatal Choice* suggests ways that we can keep our friends from committing suicide. Be a friend to these people. Reach out to them. Encourage them to talk. If you detect a problem, go to a teacher or parent and tell them. Also, familiarize yourself with the signs and symptoms of depression and suicidal behavior. Write a research report about suicide or another topic from this unit. In your report include ways to help people who are facing these problems.

4. Invite a police officer or professional counselor to your class to share their experiences and advice about suicide, drugs, alcoholism, and other topics.

RESOURCE BOOKS—MORRIS

Alateen-Hope for Children of Alcoholics. New York: Al-Anon Family Group Headquarters, Inc., 1973.

Baucom, John Q. *Fatal Choice: The Teenage Suicide Crisis.* Chicago: Moody Press, 1986.

Elkind, David. *All Grown Up & No Place to Go: Teenagers in Crisis.* Reading, Massachusetts: Addison-Wesley Publishing Co., 1984.

Hartley, Fred. *Growing Pains: First Aid for Teenagers.* Old Tappan, New Jersey, 1981.

Johnston, Jerry. *Why Suicide?* Nashville, Tennessee: Oliver Nelson Books, 1987.

Morris, Harold. *Beyond the Barriers: Overcoming Hard Times Through Tough Faith.* Pomona, California: Focus on the Family Publishing, 1987.

Morris, Harold, and Dianne Barker. *Twice Pardoned: An Ex-Con Talks to Parents and Teens.* Arcadia, California: Focus on the Family Publishing, 1986.

Neff, Pauline. *Tough Love: How Parents Can Deal with Drug Abuse.* Nashville, Tennessee: Abingdon, 1982.

Rubin, Theodore Isaac. *Overcoming Indecisiveness: The Eight Stages of Effective Decisionmaking.* New York: Harper & Row, 1985.

Sanders, Bill. *Tough Turf: A Teen Survival Manual.* Old Tappan, New Jersey: Fleming H. Revell Co., 1986.

Strack, Jay. *Drugs and Drinking: What Every Teen and Parent Should Know.* Nashville, Tennessee: Thomas Nelson, Inc., 1985.

Winn, Marie. rev. ed. *The Plug-In Drug: Television, Children, and the Family.* New York: Viking Penguin, Inc., 1985.

WALK FROM HARDSHIP TO CHAMPIONSHIP

JESSE OWENS

"I didn't look at the end of the pit. I decided I wasn't going to come down. I was going to fly. I was going to stay up in the air forever.

I began my run, also fast from the beginning, not gradual like most, but then faster. I went faster, precariously fast, using all my speed to its advantage. And then!

"I hit the take-off board. Leaped up, up, up . . . My body was weightless . . . I surged with all I had but at the same time merely let it float . . . higher . . . higher . . . into the clouds . . . I was reaching for the clouds . . . the clouds . . . the heavens.

"I was coming down! Back to earth. I fought against it. I kicked my legs. I churned my arms. I reached to the sky as I leaped for the farthest part of the ground. The farthest—I was on the earth once again.

"Luz was the first to reach me. 'You did it! I know you did it,' he whispered. They measured. I had done it. I had gone farther than Luz. I had set a new Olympic record. I had jumped farther than any man on earth."

BIOGRAPHICAL SKETCH

James Cleveland "Jesse" Owens was a grandson of slaves and one of seven children who grew up in a cotton-growing community. He learned to read and write in a one-room school where he could attend only when it wasn't cotton-picking time. Due to lack of money for a doctor's care, Jesse almost bled to death at the age of five. No matter how poor and hungry his family had been the week before, Jesse's family walked the nine miles back from church, talking about their dreams. Jesse's dream was to go to college.

When Jesse was nine, his family moved to Cleveland with new hope for a better life. In the fourth grade he fell in love with his classmate Ruth, whom he later married. In the fifth grade he met Charles Riley, coach of the high school track team, who believed Jesse would go to the Olympics someday. His family couldn't afford any equipment, so he ran and ran. He loved to run, because it was something he could do all by himself under his own power. Every morning Jesse got up with the sun, ate breakfast, and exercised. After school, he held different jobs. Jesse increasingly worked to run faster, and his name soon appeared in the newspapers and record books.

Jesse received several scholarship offers from across the country, and he asked his coach's advice. Coach Riley said Jesse should not accept any of them, and he should pay his own way. When Jesse entered Ohio State University, he asked for only one thing in return for giving up the scholarships. If a job opened up on campus, they would give his father a job. On May 25, 1935, during the Big Ten Track Championship in Ann Arbor, Michigan, Jesse broke five world records and tied one in less than an hour, although he was suffering from a bad back.

In the early 1830's, his ancestors were brought on a boat across the Atlantic Ocean from Africa to America as slaves. In August of 1936, Jesse boarded a boat to go back across the Atlantic Ocean to do battle with Adolf Hitler, a man who thought men should be slaves to him and his Aryan armies. Hitler was gone as Jesse joined his teammates on the victory stand with a fourth gold medal around his neck. Tears came to his eyes as the U.S. flag was raised and the national anthem was played. *"I felt great patriotism and a great sense of accomplishment,"* he recalled. *"It was the most marvelous moment of my life."* In his honor, his granddaughter carried the Olympic torch into the Los Angeles Coliseum for the opening ceremony of the 1984 Olympics.

CREATIVE ENCOUNTER #1 .... Risk-Taking and Friendship

At the 1936 Olympic Games held in Berlin, the Nazi dictator Adolf Hitler wanted to prove that his Aryan race was superior to any other in the world. Jesse had fouled twice and had only one more trial to qualify for the broad jump. His major rival Luz Long of Germany offered Jesse advice that helped him qualify for the final. It took a lot of courage for the German to comfort and counsel the American Black in full view of Hitler. Hitler hurriedly left when Jesse broke the Olympic record.

"I didn't know how to thank Luz Long. Because of him, because of his seeing past skin color, nationality, and Hitler's godless beliefs, I had what was the most important to me in the world: a chance to rise from Oakville to champion of the entire world.

"All I could offer in return was my friendship. Luz turned out to be the best friend I ever had. He turned out to be what you might call a messenger from God."

Friendship often involves risks as we see in the lives of Luz and Jesse. To be vulnerable can be a risk. Openness and sharing disappointments, weaknesses, and failures involve trust that your friend will not use or hold against you what you have shared. What risks have you taken or have you seen others experience in standing by a friend?_____

_____

_____

Write qualities in the gold medal that are needed to build and maintain a committed friendship. Think of the friendship of Jesse and Luz to help you think of these qualities.

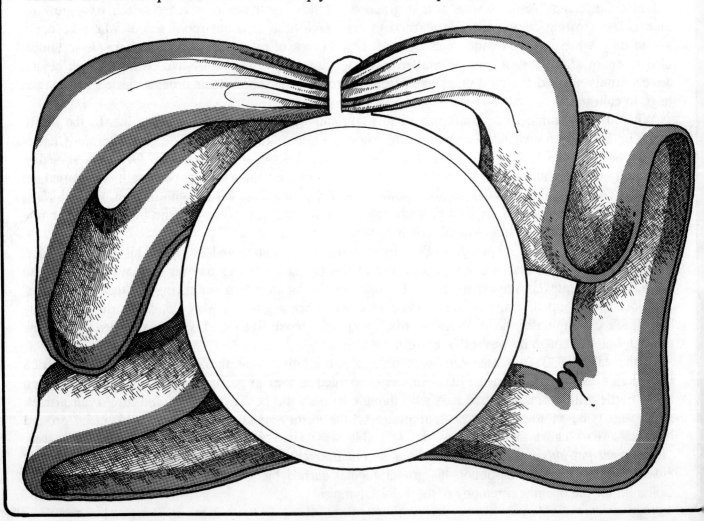

CREATIVE ENCOUNTER #2 . . . . Lack of Commitment

After breaking records in the 1936 Olympics, Jesse returned to New York to be welcomed by the mayor, who had a convertible car ready for him to ride through the streets lined with people. Celebrities and millionaires gave him parties. Millionaires offered him jobs, but then did not follow through with their offers. When he got back to Cleveland, only one job was offered—a local playground instructor for twenty-eight dollars a week. When Jesse confronted tax troubles and financial crises, his friends turned away.

"My family stuck by me, but they were just about the only ones. Walking out in the streets which I used to love so much became torture. The kids never changed. They yelled my name and waved like always. But the grown-ups, they were beyond belief.

"People I didn't know but who knew Jesse Owens, shunning me. People who knew me well, looking the other way like they didn't see. And the phone—the phone that always had to have three buttons on it because so many calls came in at once—became like another piece of soundless furniture."

Being deserted by a friend when you need him most is very painful. Commitment is an important ingredient in a friendship. We often want the pleasure of deep friendships, but not the responsibilities. Commitment costs. There is much giving and self-sacrifice. Loyalty means I will not desert my friend or withdraw my acceptance and care. Friendship takes hard work. We need to make sure we are doing our part to maintain relationships.

Why do you think there is a lack of commitment in relationships? How does selfishness play a part in lack of commitment? What problems arise when there is a lack of commitment? Working through is harder than walking out. Comment on this statement. Why is it best to work through rather than walk out?

CREATIVE ENCOUNTER #3 . . . . Commitment and Sports

Coach Tom Landry states in *The Commitment of Champions*, *"Personal excellence involves an individual commitment to seek perfection, to be the absolute best we can be in whatever we do. It embraces every aspect of our lives and challenges us to reach beyond our perceived limitations in order to find the achievement that rewards maximum effort. It is self-imposed adversity.*

"Such commitment can be seen everywhere. But nowhere is it more visibly dramatic than in athletics, where men and women endure pain and hardship to realize individual and team excellence. Their stories of triumph in the face of adversity, and in spite of great personal sacrifice, are models of human endeavor."

Give an oral presentation about the role that commitment plays in the sports world. Interweave your thoughts about Tom Landry's statements about commitment throughout your presentation.

CREATIVE ENCOUNTER #4 .... Building Friendships

In Luz's last letter to Jesse, Luz asked Jesse to go to Germany and find his son Karl and tell him about his father. Luz Long was killed in war fighting for Germany.

"And I paid one other 'debt,' though I received much more in return. I returned to Berlin and made good my vow to see Luz Long one more time. I saw Luz in the face of his son Karl.

"We walked, we talked. We looked at the sights of Berlin together. We went to the place where, in 1936, Luz's name and my own had been inscribed, supposedly for all time, in metal. Our names were still there, but next to them were bullet holes. The bullets which made those holes were no different than the one which struck down my brother, Luz Long."

In his book *The Friendship Factor*, Alan Loy McGinnis suggests five rules for deepening friendships. *"Assign top priority to your relationships. Cultivate transparency. Dare to talk about your affection. Learn the gestures of love. Create space in your relationships."* State specific goals under each statement to help you deepen your friendships. The following are examples:

Commitment means I will stick by my friend even when he has failed. Trustworthiness means I will not gossip about my friend or tell his secrets.

Commitment means I will _____

Self-sacrifice means I will _____

Loyalty means I will _____

Trustworthiness means I will_____

Being a good friend means I will be someone who is able to both reveal who I am and to listen to the other person.

Being a good friend means I will be someone who_____

_____

A friend is a companion who will lighten the load of your heaviest burdens.

A friend is someone who willingly accepts you for who you really are.

A friend is _____

A friend is _____

A friend is _____

106

CREATIVE ENCOUNTER #5 ....Commitment and You

Charles R. Swindoll, noted author and communicator, talks about commitment in his book *Strike the Original Match.*

"*Ours is a runaway world. Runaway teenagers. Runaway athletes. Runaway students. Runaway wives and husbands. Unlike our forefathers—who toughed it out regardless—when the going gets rough, we look for a way out, not a way through.*

"*Listen again to the word:* **commitment**. *Commitment is the key.*

"The 1980 Winter Olympics ended yesterday. A group of kids (all in their teens and early 20's) have startled the athletic world.

"How did they do it? Honestly now, what turned the American dream to gold?

"Those confident kids from the Midwest and East didn't rely on rabbit-in-the-hat tricks to win. They faced veteran finesse teams, one after another, with a game plan as old as hockey itself: Never back down, never quit, hang tough, keep hammering away, stay at it, regardless.

"In a word: **commitment**."

Think about these questions. How does the word *commitment* fit in your own life? What role does commitment play with your family and friends? How is commitment important with setting your goals and developing your philosophy in life? What people, goals, and philosophy are you committed to?

Write in the doors what you are planning to do to stay accountable to your commitments. Include what you would like to do to improve and strengthen your relationships and commitments in each area of your life: family, friends, and goals.

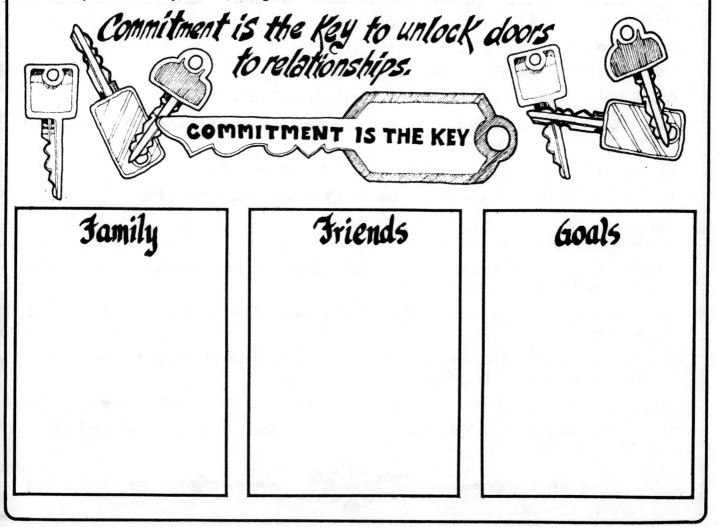

Commitment is the key to unlock doors to relationships.

COMMITMENT IS THE KEY

Family	Friends	Goals

INDEPENDENT PROJECTS—OWENS

1. Make a booklet showing how the quality of commitment is portrayed in the lives of champions throughout sports history. Choose such committed champions as Julius Erving, Walter Payton, Andre Thorton, or Earl Campbell.
2. Jesse Owens has been an inspiration to Carl and Carol Lewis. On Carol's seventeenth birthday, she won a gold medal for the long jump in West Berlin's Olympic Stadium, where Jesse Owens jumped forty-four years earlier. Carl Lewis had publicly announced his intent to repeat Jesse Owen's 1936 record win of four gold medals, and his dream came true at the 1984 Olympics. Compare and contrast how the historical events affected the Olympics during Jesse Owen's participation in the 1936 Olympics in Berlin to the time when Carol Lewis competed in Berlin. Include your opinions about the U.S. team not being able to compete in the 1980 Olympics in Moscow and the Soviet boycott of the 1984 Olympics in Los Angeles.
3. Make a chart of the records and achievements of Jesse Owens or another champion. Find out what kind of schedule and exercise program that athlete was committed to that paved his/her way to success.
4. You are making a firm commitment when you begin an exercise program. Plan your own schedule of commitment to exercise with a variety of activities.
5. Make a list of ways you can become closer to people and deepen your friendships. Base your information on *The Friendship Factor*.

RESOURCE BOOKS—OWENS

The Associated Press. *Pursuit of Excellence, The Olympic Story.* Danbury, Connecticut: Grolier Enterprises, Inc., 1983.

Eble, Diane. *I.D.* Wheaton, Illinois: Tyndale House Publishers, Inc., 1987.

Girardi, Wolfgang. *Olympic Games.* New York: Franklin Watts, Inc., 1972.

Glass, Bill, and Mike Koehler. *The Commitment of Champions.* Dallas: Bill Glass Evangelistic Association, 1984.

Kaufman, Mervyn. *Jesse Owens.* New York: Thomas Y. Crowell Co., 1973.

Kettelkamp, Larry. *Bill Cosby: Family Funny Man.* New York: Simon and Schuster, 1987.

Kieran, John, and Arthur Daley. *The Story of the Olympic Games, 776 B.C. to 1968.* rev. ed. New York: J.B. Lippincott Co., 1969.

McGinnis, Alan Loy. *The Friendship Factor: How to Get Closer to the People You Care For.* Minneapolis: Augsburg Publishing House, 1979.

Owens, Jesse, and Paul Neimark. *Jesse: The Man Who Outran Hitler.* Plainfield, New Jersey: Logos International, 1978.

Rust, Art, Jr., and Edna Rust. *Art Rust's Illustrated History of the Black Athlete.* Garden City, New York: Doubleday & Co., Inc., 1985.

Walsh, John. *The Summer Olympics.* 4th ed., rev. Frank Litsky. New York: Franklin Watts, Inc., 1979.

Wendel, Tim. *Going for the Gold: How the U.S. Won at Lake Placid.* Westport, Connecticut: Lawrence Hill & Co., 1980.

WALK FROM OBSCURITY TO ROYALTY

DALE EVANS ROGERS

"Kids! Roy loved kids. I think that was the first real spark that flashed between us, the first bond of common interest. All my life I had wanted kids, a lot of kids. Roy was always interested in children—particularly sick and handicapped children. My eyes would fill up when I would see him climb down from the saddle to put his hand on the head of some little crippled kid. Sick ones, lonely ones, poor ones, have received calls from him, personal visits in hospital rooms, or invitations to the ranch for the weekend.

"Believe me, though, ours is not a 'they rode off into the sunset and lived happily ever after' story. Three times Roy and I have felt the painful laceration of death as we stood, crushed, by the graveside of our children. To call these 'hard times' seems the understatement of the century. These were intensely human moments for me. The deep hurt seared through my body like a rampaging forest fire in our California mountains."

BIOGRAPHICAL SKETCH

Dale could sing before she could read or write. In her early teens she found herself married and deserted, left to support a baby boy. She struggled through years of wracking loneliness and discouragement from little local radio stations to big-name bands, determined to be a good mother and to become a professional singer, if it cost her life. It nearly did just that before she made it to California and Republic Studios.

Dale made her first film debut in 1943 in *Swing Your Partner*. She was featured in several films, including a western with John Wayne. The following year she acted for the first time opposite Republic's singing cowboy star Roy Rogers in *The Cowboy and the Senorita*. Most of the many motion pictures, in which Dale has played have been westerns with songs and have costarred Roy and Trigger, "the smartest horse in the movies." Before going to Hollywood, Dale had not been on a horse since childhood, but as Roy's leading lady she became an accomplished equestrienne.

Dale and Roy moved into television with *The Roy Rogers Show* in 1951. Singing their theme song, "Happy Trails to You," one of Dale's own compositions, Dale and Roy became heroes to children across America. In their rodeo and arena appearances, they are noted for their colorful costumes and elaborate professional accessories. Every commercial product Dale and Roy endorsed was tested on their own children before it hit the public. They had Roy Rogers milk glasses, curtains, boots, holsters, tents, school lunch boxes, and many other novelties.

When Roy married Dale, her new "family" included three children, thirty hunting dogs, innumerable horses, and more than two hundred homing pigeons. Altogether, there were nine children in their multicultural family, and they lived on their Double R Bar Ranch.

The King of the Cowboys and Queen of the West are a legend in their own lifetimes. They have opened doors of hope for suffering children and stricken parents. Dale has held abused, orphaned, and retarded children in her arms; Roy has lifted blind and lame "buckaroos" to sit on Trigger's saddle, as he talked to them about courage.

Dale is a sparkling celebrity, actress-singer, TV and radio personality, best-selling author, and speaker. Futhermore, their son Roy, Jr., honors her saying, *"She's everybody's sister, everybody's mom. In a sense, that's because if she's anything, she's a mother."*

CREATIVE ENCOUNTER #1 . . . . Heroic Footsteps

"My childhood hero was my Granddaddy Wood of Uvalde, Texas. Even though I was quite young at the time, Granddaddy left an indelible imprint on my life that has remained vivid over the years. For me, he has been a model of selfless caring for other people."

Many heroes are people who are living very ordinary lives, but are doing so in heroic ways. Their names are not up in lights or in headlines.

Listen to their footsteps. The protective footsteps of a single mother are ever-so-quiet, as she tiptoes to the crib of her sick baby in the hush of the night. Careful, hesitant footsteps edge toward the curb of a street with the loyal, trained footsteps of a dog to guide his blind master. Listen to a grandfather's wise, shuffling footsteps followed by the pitter-patter of his grandchild's carefree, lively footsteps.

As you tread behind your heroes and observe their heroic deeds, their footprints will be firmly planted in your heart. Moreover, you will make new footprints of your own.

To express why you admire these hometown heroes, write two or more adjectives beside each set of footprints to describe their heroic footsteps. Use these descriptions in a poem or a composition about following the footsteps of your heroes. Salute your heroes by giving them a copy of your writing.

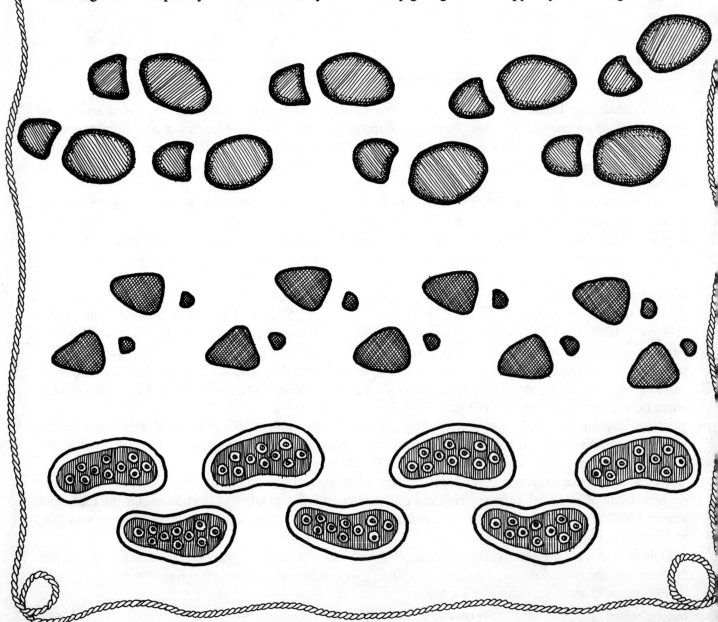

CREATIVE ENCOUNTER #2 .... A Parade of Heroes

"It was the morning of New Year's Day, 1977, and the traditional Tournament of Roses Parade had again turned Pasadena into a wild celebration of sight and sound. There, amidst the marching bands, the prize-winning flower-draped floats, the gaily costumed riders and baton-twirling majorettes, the King of Cowboys and Queen of the West were clearly the centerpieces of the celebration.

"They represented much to many. To some they were still Saturday afternoon heroes, a welcome reminder of younger days when there were, indeed, still heroes. To others, they were living monuments to the good which is still so much a part of the American Way."

Who are your heroes that are public figures? Celebrate a tribute to your heroes.

Draw a parade of illustrations to represent your heroes. A cowboy hat and boots or a personalized cattle brand could represent Roy Rogers. Choose one of your favorite heroes. On the back of this page, draw a float, especially designed for your hero to ride in a parade.

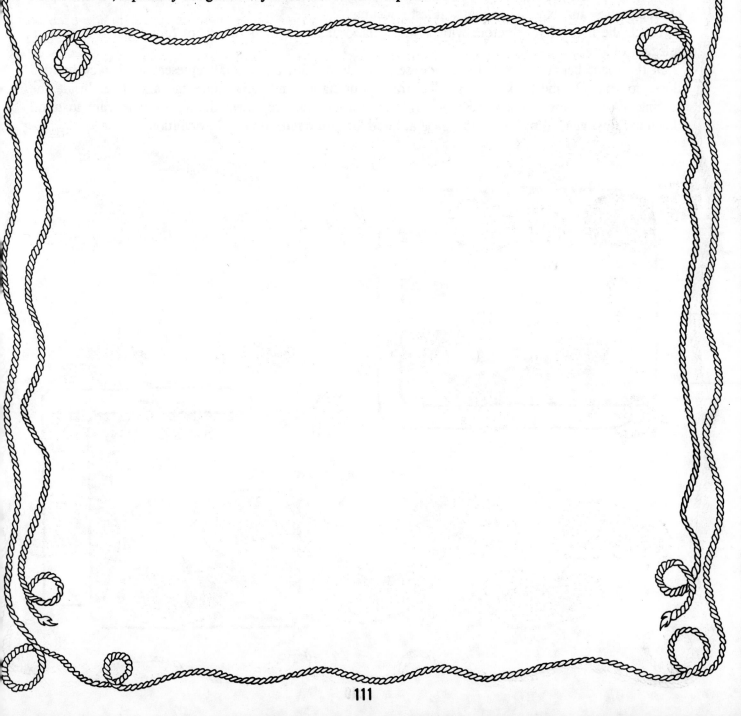

CREATIVE ENCOUNTER #3 . . . . *Hand*ing Down a Legacy

"There is always time for frequent visits from all the grandchildren and great-grandchildren. What those children have inherited is a legacy they share with an entire nation.

"Roy and Dale continue to be loved and admired. That affection is not only what they are and who they are, but for what they represent.

"A legacy indeed! It is an example that any child, or any nation, would do well to follow."

Reflect upon the legacy that Roy, Dale, and famous and hometown heroes have **hand**ed down to us. Our grandparents have **hand**ed us a legacy of **hand**made memories, priceless **hand**-me-downs, and treasured gifts of their **hand**iwork.

On the other **hand**, take a few moments to picture yourself as a hero to others. What legacy do you want to **hand** down to your children and future generations? How will you leave them a part of you? How will you equip them to **hand**le adversity? Your legacy will include a **hand**ful of examples, characteristics, and experiences that will last a lifetime.

Touch the lives of your heroes with a warm **hand**shake. Hold the **hand**s of future generations with a legacy of love.

In the space below, write words or phrases, and draw illustrations that represent the legacy **hand**ed down to you. On the back of this page, trace your **hand**, and write your age and date. Inside the tracing of your **hand**, write words and draw illustrations that represent the legacy you want to **hand** down to future generations. Keep this page at **hand** for future reflection and evaluation.

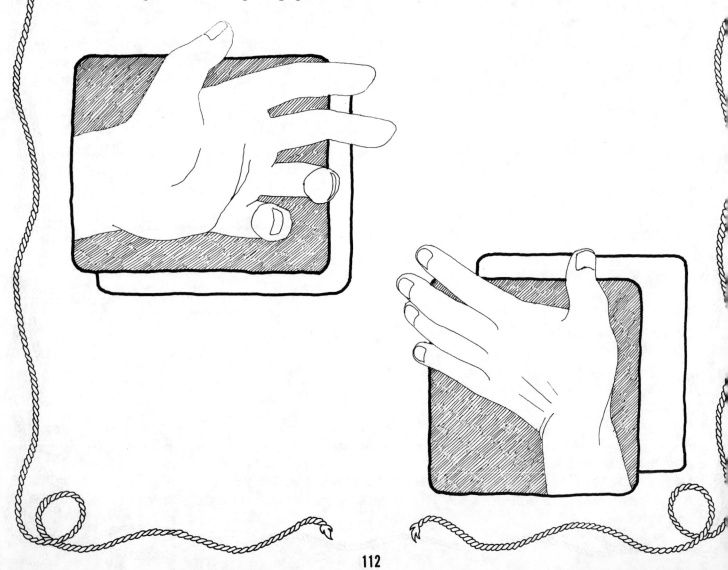

"The Western mood is caught immediately by visitors as they enter the picturesque log stockade structure which encloses the Roy Rogers-Dale Evans Museum. They relive those cowboy days of an earlier West just as if they were a part of them. Their imaginations and spirit of adventure reach a high pitch at the sight of horses and stage coaches and action scenes from our early Western movies."

Follow the trail to gripping frontier adventure with the Queen of the West and the King of the Cowboys. Nightfall is approaching, and it's time to settle down after a long day on horseback. Listen to these stories about Roy and Dale around a crackling, warm campfire on a starlit night.

One afternoon as the cast was waiting for the shooting of a scene, they were all sitting around listening to one of Gabby Hayes' delightfully funny stories. Dale was already on her horse, ready to ride whenever the director was. When Gabby delivered his punch line, she broke into laughter and inadvertently dug her heels into her horse's side. The horse bolted. He was running wild at a full gallop, and Dale was hanging onto the saddle horn for dear life, screaming.

Now the story begins to sound like it came directly from the pages of one of their scripts. Roy jumped on Trigger and came after Dale, riding up alongside and grabbing her just as she was about to tumble ankle over elbow into the hot sands of the California desert. Hero saves heroine!

Trigger had an entire repertoire of tricks, some of which were dancing the carioca, walking nearly a hundred feet on his hind legs, playing dead, and drinking milk from a bottle, unaided. Wearing special cushioned shoes, Roy's golden palomino even pranced into the lobby of the Dixie Hotel in New York, took a pencil in his mouth, and registered with a big X.

In the arena shows and rodeos, Roy had an act about the cowboy and his loyal horse. The announcer painted a word picture about the cowboy riding through outlaw-infested country, in danger of being shot at any time.

Roy galloped out on Trigger, and suddenly a shot rang out. Roy slumped in his saddle, but Trigger kept running. Then a second shot rang out. Trigger stumbled a bit then started running again, this time limping because one of his legs was wounded. He limped along like that for 25 or 30 feet, getting weaker and weaker, and then he went down.

Roy rolled out of the saddle and lay along side of him. Someone played "Taps," and the lights went out briefly so Roy could get back on Trigger and they could take a bow.

Now that you are more acquainted with these western personalities, lace fact with fiction, and write your own adventurous stories for the Roy Rogers television series. Decide what parts you and your friends will play. Put your script into action with western costumes, background music, sound effects, and props. Videotape your western.

Setting: Mineral City, located in Paradise Valley

Plot: Friendship and a combining of efforts solve the problems and right the wrongs in each episode.

Theme Song: "Happy Trails" by Dale Evans Rogers

Characters: Roy Rogers, the prosperous owner of the Double R Bar Ranch

   Dale, proprietor of the local Eureka Cafe

   Trigger and Buttermilk, Roy and Dale's horses

   Bullet, their educated German shepherd

   Pat Brady, Roy's comic sidekick

   Nellybelle, Pat Brady's ornery jeep

A hidden stuntman inside the jeep made it look as though Nellybelle was driving herself. Pat Brady often moaned, "Whoa, Nellybelle!"

Other Characters: the helpless townsfolk, the villain, the town brat, wranglers

A Working Crew: script writers; a producer; a director; people to manage the sound, cameras, props, and costumes.

"As a new stepmother to the three little Rogerses, the going was rough for me at first. But time and experience have taught me a priceless lesson: Any child you take for your own becomes your own if you give of yourself to that child. I have borne two children and had seven others by adoption, and they are all my children, equally beloved and precious."

Let's turn the pages of Dale's family picture album, and make their family memories come alive. As a single mother, Dale had raised her first son Tom from a previous marriage. Dale authored a book of letters to Tom.

Cheryl, the oldest of Roy's three, was adopted. Then Linda Lou, their little "buckarina," arrived. When their son was born, radio stations and newspapers all over the country announced, "The King of the Cowboys Has a Prince!" Roy Rogers, Jr., Dusty, never knew his real mother; she died six days after he was born.

Turn another page of their picture album and meet Robin, Roy and Dale's own baby girl. As a Down's syndrome baby, highly susceptible to illness, Robin caught the mumps. She was buried on her second birthday. Dale wrote a book about Robin called *Angel Unaware*. It has comforted thousands of families with children like Robin and has challenged the world to be compassionate.

On Dusty's sixth birthday, Dale and Roy brought two new adopted children home. Black-haired, little Dodie was of Indian, Scottish and Irish descent. When five-year-old Sandy first saw Roy, he held out his hand and drawled, "Howdy, Partner!"

Sandy was abandoned by his alcoholic parents. He suffered from malnutrition, brain damage, and several physical handicaps, because he had been badly treated and abused. His great passion as a child was to play "soldier"; thus, he enlisted in the army. At a party in Germany, he drank a lot of liquor, which killed him. Sandy, who had wanted so much to fight for his country, had been killed, not by an enemy, but by the taunts of "friends" who challenged him to "drink like a man." In memory of their son and in fulfillment of his dream, Dale and Roy volunteered to perform for American servicemen in Vietnam.

On a visit to a Scottish orphanage, Roy and Dale met eleven-year-old Marion. They brought her to America, and she became a permanent member of their international family.

Turn another page of their picture album, and meet another newcomer to their family. Debbie, a Korean-Puerto Rican, was a Korean War orphan. A trip to visit an orphanage in Mexico was part of Debbie's twelfth birthday celebration. Coming home, the church bus full of children had an accident, and promising, talented Debbie was killed.

Robin, Sandy, and Debbie are not closed pages in their family picture album. Their lives are written upon Roy and Dale's hearts. They inspired Roy and Dale into a new vocation of compassion for sick, neglected, and underprivileged children around the world.

Family traditions keep the pages in family picture albums alive. Traditions are memory links that bind together the generations. Mix family time and togetherness. Stir with traditions to create homemade memories.

What are your family traditions? Make your own happy memories with family traditions. For a birthday celebration, write fun messages on several notes. Give a written clue on each note, directing the person to the next note. Hide the cards. The last note will direct him to a surprise gift. Capture those precious moments with a camera, and keep your memories alive with your own family picture album.

Research traditions of other countries. Present to your class ideas for family traditions to build family togetherness.

CREATIVE ENCOUNTER #6 . . . . A Collection of Recollections

Beautiful memories are homemade. Special memories of yesterday were once moments of today. Recalling those fond, indelible memories gives strength to sustain us for today. The past is a foundation on which we must build for tomorrow.

The Roy Rogers-Dale Evans Museum takes you on a journey down their "happy trails" with a fascinating collection of photographs, family mementoes, show business memorabilia, scrapbook materials, and displays. Corral the nostalgia of yesterday from your mental scrapbook. Take a sentimental journey down those "happy trails" of your life, as people and places step out of the shadows to visit you.

Imagine having your own perpetuating family museum with the cherished collectibles handed down from generation to generation. Draw a potpourri of illustrations throughout your museum that represent some of your precious memories.

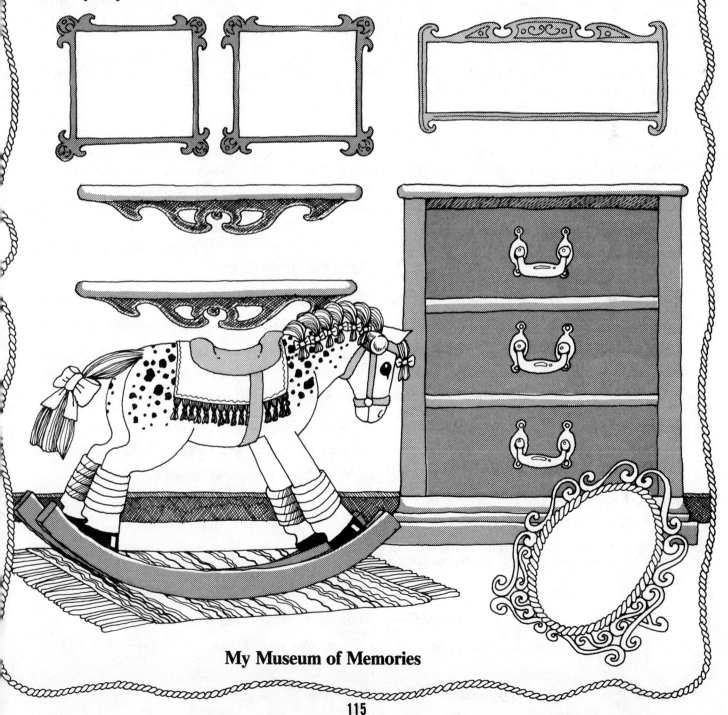

My Museum of Memories

INDEPENDENT PROJECTS—ROGERS

1. Roy often visited seriously ill children, and he cut several records to be played for unusual cases during necessary therapy. Research the field of music therapy and the importance and effects of music.

2. *"How sad to write a song for somebody after he's gone and can't appreciate it. Why can't Dad have a song of his own, right now?"* Roy Rogers, Jr., wrote a song about the kind and gentle living legend. Compose a song for someone important to you.

3. *"Robin is a very special baby. She's not very strong, and she's going to be slower than other babies are. We have to take care of Robin just as though she were a delicate little flower."* Dale explained Robin's needs to her other children. Write about Robin, their Down's syndrome baby, and the characteristics and sensitive concerns of mental retardation.

4. The Roy Rogers Riders Clubs were lauded as weapons against juvenile delinquency. The clubs suggested ways for his fans to do hospital, charity, and civic work and also dealt effectively with accident prevention and safety measures. Form a club with similar goals. Find ways to help needy children.

5. *"Latch-key kids. Hired baby-sitters. Working mothers. Divorce. Remarriage. Stepchildren. Death. Hollywood. Fame. Any one of these elements can, and often does, provide ample climate for child abuse, juvenile delinquency, rebellion or misery."* Roy Rogers, Jr., states that these odds were against their family. Interweave how their family overcame the odds with your own research about any of the preceding topics.

6. Plan a Western Day, featuring a parade of heroes.

RESOURCE BOOKS—ROGERS

Rogers, Dale Evans. *Angel Unaware.* Old Tappan, New Jersey: Fleming H. Revell Co., 1953.

_____ . *Cool It or Lose It! Dale Evans Rogers Raps with Youth.* Old Tappan, New Jersey: Fleming H. Revell Co., 1972.

_____ . *Dale: My Personal Picture Album.* Old Tappan, New Jersey: Fleming H. Revell Co., 1971.

_____ . *Dearest Debbie: In Ai Lee.* Old Tappan, New Jersey: Fleming H. Revell Co., 1965.

_____ . *Salute to Sandy.* Old Tappan, New Jersey: Fleming H. Revell Co., 1967.

_____ . *To My Son: Faith at Our House.* Old Tappan, New Jersey: Fleming H. Revell Co., 1957.

_____ . *The Woman at the Well.* Old Tappan, New Jersey: Fleming H. Revell Co., 1970.

Rogers, Dale Evans, and Carole C. Carlson. *Grandparents Can.* Old Tappan, New Jersey: Fleming H. Revell Co., 1983.

Rogers, Dale Evans, and Frank S. Mead. *Hear the Children Crying: The Child Abuse Epidemic.* Old Tappan, New Jersey: Fleming H. Revell Co., 1978.

_____ . *Let Freedom Ring!* Old Tappan, New Jersey: Fleming H. Revell Co., 1975.

Rogers, Roy, Jr. *Growing Up with Roy and Dale.* Ventura, California: Regal Books, 1986.

Stowers, Carlton. *Happy Trails: The Story of Roy Rogers and Dale Evans.* Waco, Texas: Word Books, 1979.

GALE SAYERS

"The Lord is first, my friends are second, and I am third. It held a lot of meaning for me. And, if you think about it, it is a good philosophy of life. I try to live by it. Sometimes it's hard. I don't live by it all the time, I know, but keeping that saying close to me helps bring me back, keeps me from straying too far from that philosophy.

"He has the heart of a giant and that rare form of courage that allows him to kid himself and his opponent, cancer. He has the mental attitude that makes me proud to have a friend who spells out the word **courage** *twenty-four hours a day of his life.*

"You flatter me by giving me this award, but I tell you here and now that I accept it for Brian Piccolo. Brian Piccolo is the man of courage who should receive the George S. Halas award. It is mine tonight; it is Brian Piccolo's tomorrow . . . . I love Brian Piccolo and I'd like all of you to love him, too. Tonight when you hit your knees, please ask God to love him . . . ."

BIOGRAPHICAL SKETCH

Gale grew up with his parents fighting and drinking, not enough food in the house, cockroaches running over things, and no heat in the winter. He didn't realize he grew up in the ghetto until he moved away from it. Gale learned from his experience that if you want to make it bad enough, no matter how bad it is you can make it.

When Gale was eight years old, he ran track, played basketball and baseball. Football was his favorite sport. He thinks the sense of competition gave him the drive for football, always wanting to be the best. In grade school they played "flag" football in the street, alley, empty lot, or local park. Other kids their age might be in real trouble—fighting, robbing, and taking drugs, but Gale and his friends would be practicing and playing football until ten or eleven at night.

As a senior at Central High School in Omaha, Nebraska, he scored 108 points in football, breaking the intercity scoring record. Their team went undefeated. One of the reasons he enjoyed scoring so many touchdowns was that it kept him from going hungry in a difficult year at home. A local drive-in gave him a double-decker hamburger for every touchdown he scored.

Gale received many offers to colleges, and he decided to attend the University of Kansas with a football scholarship. Gale said his proudest achievement in college was not making All-American in his junior and senior years or setting a Big Eight career rushing record. It was making a three-point average right before his senior year.

After college Gale signed a contract with George Halas, owner of the Chicago Bears. The Bears called Gale "Magic." Having suffered a severe knee injury in 1968, this Chicago Bears running back returned the following season after much perseverance, hard work, and exercise. At the end of that year, Gale's 1,032 yards were the best in the NFL. His six-year superstar career with the Bears generated many honors, such as becoming a member of the Pro Football Hall of Fame in 1977.

Today Gale is Vice President of Computer Supplies by Sayers, and his family resides in Northbrook, Illinois. In 1968, Gale set up a foundation to give clothes and scholarships to young newspaper carriers. He worked with the "Reach Out" program in Chicago and taught young people in the ghetto how to play football. Gale has been Athletic Director at universities, and he loves being around students, listening to and helping them with their problems. Gale has achieved greatness, both on and off the football field.

CREATIVE ENCOUNTER #1 . . . . Deepening Friendships

"It's ironic the way things happen. Because of my injury and my mental state afterward, I got to know Pick even better and became closer to him than almost anybody else on the team. And then when he became ill, it seemed that our friendship deepened, and we got to understand each other even better. And that's when I found out what a beautiful person he really was."

Gale Sayers was to be given the George S. Halas Award as the most courageous player in pro football at the Professional Football Writers annual dinner. Gale tearfully accepted the award for Brian Piccolo, who was confined to his bed at home. Alan Loy McGinnis states in his book, *The Friendship Factor,* *"But how much more enriched our lives could be if we dared to declare our affection as Sayers did that night in New York. Rule number three for deepening your friendships is: Dare to talk about your affection."*

Draw a symbol that represents friendship. Write a motto that signifies the importance of friendship. For example: Friendship strengthens in hardship. Think of the friendship and philosophy of Gale Sayers and Brian Piccolo to help you make up the symbol and motto.

NAME

CREATIVE ENCOUNTER #2 . . . . **Memories of a Friend**

Brian was devoted to his sister-in-law, Carol Murrath, who had cerebral palsy. Carol wrote about her memories of Brian.

"I feel very bad about Brian's death because I loved him very much. He was always good to me. Brian would take time to do things with me. We always teased each other. Brian was very sweet to all my friends at the Cerebral Palsy Center. One of the girls in my class who cannot talk typed a note saying that when her sister married she hoped he would be someone like Brian. Every time we went to a football game, Brian would make sure I had a special place and that it was easy for us to get there with the wheelchair. When I visited in Chicago, whenever possible he would introduce me to some of the players on the team. I have lost a very good friend and I will always miss him. I loved him so much."

Recall cherished memories of a friend with whom you have had to say good-bye. Maybe your friend did not die, but moved away. Reminisce for a moment, and think about your talks and fun times together. Write words to describe your friend in the sports equipment. Also, write specific things that especially remind you of your friend.

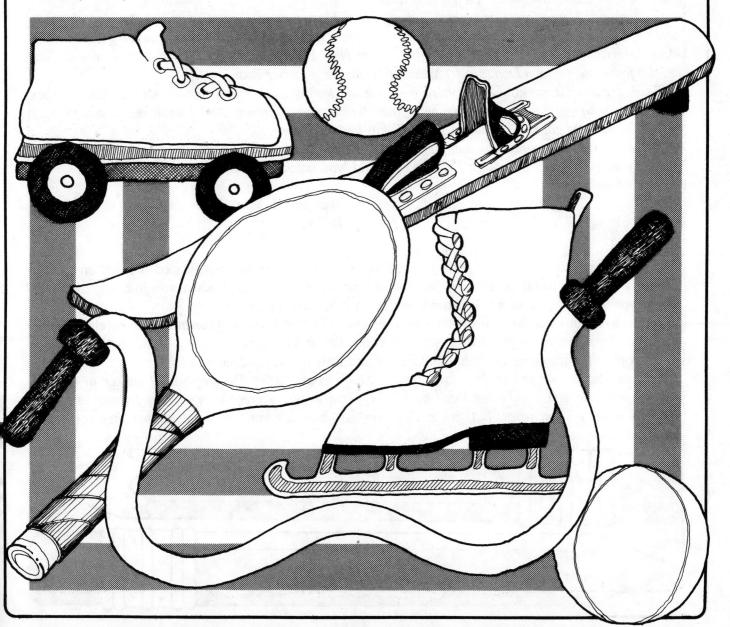

On December 6, 1969, Freddie Steinmark played in a game between the Texas Longhorns and the Arkansas Razorbacks. Freddie and the Longhorns won that game, 15-14, and the title of being national champions on the one hundredth anniversary of college football. Six days later Freddie lost his left leg to cancer. Freddie became a national symbol of determination and courage to young people struggling against cancer. He died on June 6, 1971.

Over and over again, Brian Piccolo would say to his wife, *"Joy, I've got to write Freddie Steinmark, but I just don't know how to say what I feel."* He would put if off another day, until finally the words came.

Dear Fred:

"Although I don't know you personally, we have a lot in common. This is why I'm writing you this letter. My football career, just as yours, was brought to a sudden halt this year by cancer, mine in the form of a tumor located directly below my breastbone.

"This tumor popped up from nothing to the size of a grapefruit in a period of three months. I had my surgery on November 28 at Memorial Hospital in New York and missed the last five games of the season.

"I watched your game against Arkansas from my hospital bed when I was recovering from surgery and then read about your problem a few days later.

"I guess that I, more than any other football player, know how you felt. I spent a lot of time thinking about you and praying for you in those days and that's when I decided to write. I never got to it until Mike Pyle visited my house when I got home from New York and informed me that you were a Bear fan. He found out through Don (Moon) Mullins of Houston, a former Bear.

"Fred, I guess I'd mainly like to share with you my feeling since my operation, simply that our lives are in God's hands, just as they were before our illnesses were known. And I shall never stop praying to God for the strength to carry out the plans He has laid out for me.

"I know you are a courageous young man and I hope this letter might be of some help to you. Perhaps some day we may meet one another. I'm sure we would have much to talk about.

"Best of luck to you, Fred."

> *Your friend,*
> *Brian Piccolo*

Take the time now to write a letter of comfort to a friend who has experienced a situation similar to one of yours. It could be about a time when you were disappointed when you lost a game, even though you did your best, or a time when things did not go as you planned.

Write about an event or difficult time in your own life that brought you and a friend closer. Give it to your friend as an expression of your affection. Or write a true life story or fiction story about other people who have gone through a lot together and their friendship deepened.

The narrator at the end of the movie *Brian's Song* states, *"Brian Piccolo died of cancer at the age of twenty-six. He left a wife and three daughters. He also left a great many loving friends who miss him and think of him often. But, when they think of him, it's not how he died that they remember but, rather, how he **lived**. . . How he **did** live . . . "*

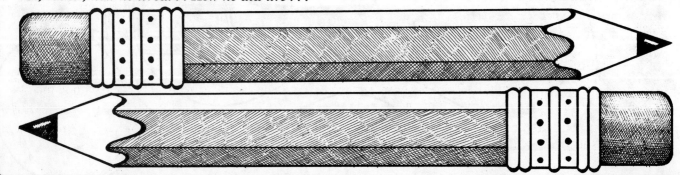

CREATIVE ENCOUNTER #4 .... Giving Yourself Away

"At one point, Pick, Concannon, Kurek, and myself went upstairs to see this little girl who had dived into a shallow swimming pool and broken her neck. She was about thirteen and was paralyzed from the neck down. She had kind of become the darling of the Bears, because every time a player came to see Dr. Fox he would send him up to see this girl. Mainly because of the girl, Brian said, he wasn't as concerned about his own troubles. The next morning, the day he left for New York, he went into the girl's room to give her a signed photograph of himself. She was asleep and he left it. Some weeks later we heard that the girl had passed away."

Sometimes when you give yourself away especially in a difficult time, you lose yourself in helping with other people's problems and forget about your own. Try to actively become involved in other people's lives. Search for someone who is hurting.

Carefully consider what you can and would like to do. Ask yourself, *"What would I need if I were in a similar situation?"* Offer specific, practical suggestions you can do for them, like, *"What can I pick up for you at the store?" "Would tomorrow be a good day to help you rake leaves?" "Would the children like to come over and play this afternoon?" "I want to help you; I'm available anytime you need me."* Make your ability a garment of service. Your willingness and your creative efforts will help your hurting friend.

Gale Sayers gave his best efforts to his friend. *"He's very, very sick and he might not ever play football again. And I think each of us should dedicate ourselves to try to give our maximum efforts to win this ball game and give the game ball to Pick. We can all sign it and take it up to him . . . ."*

Invite your friends to help you help others. This could turn into a class project that would build new bridges to reaching people in your community.

CREATIVE ENCOUNTER #5 .... Developing a Healthy Attitude

"Brian's attitude after the operation was so phenomenal it made me feel all the worse about how I had acted just after my knee surgery. The first day or two I was terrible. Pick would say something that would normally get a chuckle, and it was like I was deaf. I lay there like stone.

*"And here was Brian Piccolo, after probably the most critical moment in his whole life, in fine spirits, cool and hopeful and so positive about things. He really helped lift **your** spirits.*

"What he was really doing, I think, was carrying through the I Am Third philosophy of life. Really carrying it through. And yet it was a very positive attitude. And I think you have to be that way.

"Sometimes when you are hurting, it seems you can't help but feel sorry for yourself. Questions are asked. "Why me? Why this? Why now? Why did it happen to me especially when things were finally going great? It can't be true. I can't have cancer. I don't want to suffer."

Challenge these thoughts and replace them with coping statements. *"Okay, that's one set of thoughts. Dwelling on them just makes it worse. It did happen to me. What can I do? Where can I get help? What's the first step to recovery? What am I learning from this experience? There is no use blaming myself or anyone else. I want to focus on the present, rather than what I think could have or should have been."*

One secret of Gale and Brian's growing friendship was their sense of humor. Discuss specific incidents that demonstrate how Gale and Brian lived courageously in Gale's fight to recover from his knee injury and Brian's fight against cancer. Tell about a time when you encountered someone like Brian who actually cheered others up, while he was inflicted with terrible pain and discomfort. What do you think constitutes a healthy attitude in regard to facing cancer or another adversity?

CREATIVE ENCOUNTER #6 .... One Step at a Time

During the time of Brian's death, Gale faced so many difficult experiences at once. His parents were involved in an automobile accident. Then Gale became sick and was put into the hospital for awhile.

In the midst of depression or stress you often focus on all that has to be done and lose sight of what needs to be done now. There appears to be many tasks requiring your full attention and enormous energy. You don't know where to start, and you may feel as if you will fail miserably. All you have to do is take one more step. You may not be able to finish the task now; you can only begin now. Finishing and achieving are in the future. All you can do now is to choose to work toward your goal.

Facing the day can be too big a task. Battling cancer and all the questions about the meaning of cancer is too large of a task to tackle all at once. Focus on that first step. At any moment, you need only take one more step.

State a task or goal that seems overwhelming to you. Draw a picture to represent the task at the top of the stairsteps. Start at the bottom and list your plans on each stairstep to reach your goal. Start now to take one step at a time.

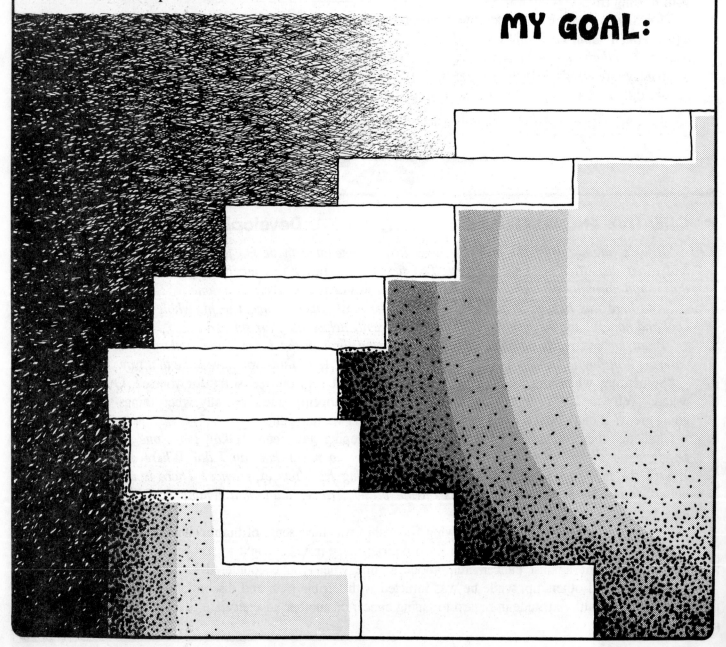

MY GOAL:

CREATIVE ENCOUNTER #7 .... Living Life to the Fullest

"I sometimes think of the similarities between new cancer patients and their families and those pioneering families who pushed West alone, into uncharted wilderness, for the sake of a goal that became increasingly difficult to recall. The perils are similar: ever-present threat of death; seemingly endless, frequently painful journeying; a host of fears that may or may not be realized; desperate effort simply to get through each day; and yet, from a marvel of inner strength, the ability to live with unforeseen risks and, somehow, take them in stride.

"With cancer, risk-taking is not foolhardy courage; it is choosing to live as fully as possible despite the disease," states Jory Graham in her book *In the Company of Others.*

Cancer. That's a scary word. The stress of cancer and cancer treatment is enormous. Risk-taking is involved in learning to live with cancer and to return to as normal a life as possible, for as long as possible, or learning to live a life without our loved one, making new friends, and finding new activities we enjoy. Our quest is to live life to the fullest in the **present.**

Sometimes it is difficult to live in the present, because there are so many worries about the past or future. What obstacles may be causing you not to live life to the fullest in the present? How would you live your life if you knew you had just a few more days to live? What would you do? What people would you want to see?

Write what living life to the fullest means to you. Make a rebus with a list of ways of how you can try to live life to the fullest.

Living life 2 the fullest means enjoying Mom's homemade 🍎🥧.
Living life 2 the fullest means relishing the beauty of a 🌅.

CREATIVE ENCOUNTER #8 .... Making Every Day Count

"My Brian was such a participant in life, every ounce and phase of it. He would make the most ordinary things special. Just taking Lori, Traci, and Kristi to buy shoes was an event, a chance to laugh and play," said Joy Piccolo, Brian's wife.

Memories of seeing someone who was so active and strong struck by this debilitating disease can come back to visit you at times when you least expect them. After a parent has cancer, the children may naturally feel that every ache or pain they have could be cancer. These fears may be somewhat normal, but try to be open and honest about your feelings to someone who cares for you. Other people can help you get the proper perspective and work through these fears.

The word *diagnosis* derives from the Greek, *gignoskein*—to know, *dia*—through and through. It is important that the physician know your loved one as through and through as possible. The family physician usually tells the family about the terminal illness, but not on the phone. Because cancer still is a mystery in many ways, sometimes it is discovered too late or misdiagnosed. This may cause feelings of misunderstanding and bitterness against a physician or others.

Forgiveness is an important ingredient in dealing with the mixture of emotions dealing with cancer. You may have to work through the emotions to forgive a doctor for a misdiagnosis, forgive the loved one who is terminally ill for being sick, or forgive yourself for the mistakes you've made in your relationship with your loved one.

While one might fear becoming pessimistic if too much is learned about the cancer, research has shown that becoming well-informed actually helps sustain hopeful attitudes. Having the facts enables patients to overcome the anxiety associated with unrealistic fears and uncertainty. The quest is to maintain a hopeful attitude and try to make every day count.

Research, write, and discuss the emotional side of cancer. Find out ways to work through these emotions.

INDEPENDENT PROJECTS—SAYERS

1. *"I was white, this guy was black. We had each traveled thousands of miles to meet in a jungle. After this night, I would never see him again. We both knew that. Yet here he was, offering to pick me up bodily and help save my life. That's a special kind of love."* Rocky Bleier was seriously wounded in Vietnam and described by the Army as 40 percent disabled, but he fought his way back to pro football to play a winning game in the Super Bowl. Read *Fighting Back*. Design a medal of honor in laudation of Rocky's courage during the scene in Vietnam and his comeback years.

2. At the peak of Lou Gehrig's career with the Yankees, he was attacked by a rare disease that robbed him of his strength. The prognosis was that he would live two to four years and the end would come suddenly and painlessly. Draw a large baseball field. Inside the diamond write about his life to depict how he left a shining legacy of courage.

3. After watching the movie *Brian's Song*, discuss the scenes throughout the development of Gale and Brian's friendship and how they came to know each other, fight each other, laugh together, and help each other.

4. Cancer is a dangerous enemy. Research the types of cancer, the causes, the symptoms, and the treatments for cancer. A good nutritious diet helps prevent cancer and is also needed as a treatment for cancer. What are other ways to prevent and treat cancer and maintain good health?

RESOURCE BOOKS—SAYERS

Bleier, Rocky, and Terry O'Neil. *Fighting Back*. New York: Stein and Day Publishers, 1975.

Blinn, William. *Brian's Song*. New York: Bantam Books, Inc., 1972.

Fiore, Neil A. *The Road Back to Health: Coping with the Emotional Side of Cancer*. New York: Bantam Books, Inc., 1984.

Graham, Frank. *Lou Gehrig: A Quiet Hero*. New York: G.P. Putnam's Sons, 1942.

Graham, Jory. *In the Company of Others: Understanding the Human Needs of Cancer Patients*. New York: Harcourt Brace Jovanovich, 1982.

Griese, Bob, and Gale Sayers. *Offensive Football*. Edited by Bill Bondurant. New York: Atheneum, 1972.

Hahn, James, and Lynn Hahn. *Sayers! The Sports Career of Gale Sayers*. Edited by Howard Schroeder. Mankato, Minnesota: Crestwood House, Inc., 1981.

Harwell, Amy, and Kristine Tomasik. *When Your Friend Gets Cancer: How You Can Help*. Wheaton, Illinois: Harold Shaw Publishers, 1987.

Kuhlman, Edward. *An Overwhelming Interference*. Old Tappan, New Jersey: Fleming H. Revell Co., 1986.

Morris, Jeannie. *Brian Piccolo: A Short Season*. New York: Rand McNally & Co., 1971.

Sayers, Gale, and Al Silverman. *I Am Third*. New York: The Viking Press, 1970.

Steinmark, Freddie. *I Play to Win*. Boston: Little, Brown and Co., 1971.

WALK FROM CRISIS TO COURAGE

JUNE SCOBEE

*"For all Americans, the shuttle tragedy was a forceful reminder of our fragile lives here on Earth and the courage of those who represent our country as the modern day pioneer, of those who roll back the unknown frontiers and give all of us new hope and new knowledge. The **Challenger 7** Mission was about learning, children and our future. The goals of that mission were diminished only if we turn away from our challenge to dedicate ourselves to the cause which our educators and space voyagers have so bravely advanced.*

"Only as we accept our problems as the challenges they really are can today's dreams become tomorrow's realities. Once we stop exploring, stop questioning, stop seeking the truth, we cease to grow. Without growth, we become complacent. With self-satisfaction, we stagnate—no longer a progressive America—and our country must continue to reach, to dream, to look forward."

June Scobee

BIOGRAPHICAL SKETCH

Being the daughter of an itinerant construction worker, June grew up in Alabama, Texas, and Florida. Because her family traveled a lot, she was forced to meet new people and make new friends. She had shared responsibility for raising her younger brothers, so she learned to solve problems on her own. June was precocious and was persistent in seeing things through. Skipping eighth grade, she graduated from high school at the age of sixteen. June enjoyed helping people and spent her extra time at school assisting other children and the teacher.

June's thirst for education led her to a doctorate degree from Texas A & M University. In 1970 she started teaching high school, then junior high, then college, then elementary school reading, and then at the university. In the summer she taught and implemented university summer presidential programs. June served as an assistant professor in gifted education at the University of Houston-Clear Lake. She is a board member of the National Association for Gifted Children. June was appointed by the governor of Texas to serve on the Space Science Industry Commission.

Her husband Dick delighted in the achievements of June. They had two children, Kathie and Richard. Dick graduated with a degree in aerospace engineering from the University of Arizona. He was the *Challenger* Space Shuttle Commander, who lost his life along with five other astronauts and school teacher Christa McAuliffe in the *Challenger* explosion on January 28, 1986.

America, washed in tears and unified by the *Challenger* disaster, gave beautiful expressions of love to the *Challenger* families. The idea of the Challenger Center came with the families' desire to give back to the American people. The *Challenger* families have designated the Challenger Center for Space Science Education as their official effort to carry on the mission and dreams of the *Challenger*. A piece of it belongs to every American. A network will be created between regional centers and those in Washington, D.C., and the Johnson Space Center. It will be a monument, not just of stone but of ideas, a place where children and teachers from across the country can come to learn the lessons that Christa McAuliffe would have taught from space and to take back to their own classrooms the excitement of space exploration. The Challenger Center is a living tribute that will link the worlds of education and exploration. June believes the best way to honor the crew is to work to honor their dreams.

CREATIVE ENCOUNTER #1 ....**A Portrait of Vision**

"What I saw in my parents was vision. We would sit and talk and look to the future. We called it picturing. Picture it better; picture the good days; picture when you grow up; picture youself as a person who will make things better; picture yourself in charge of situations where you can help others.

"Be persistent. Work hard to see that your own dreams come true, all the while holding on to your childlike spirit of adventure and curiosity."

Christa McAuliffe was an inspiring portrait of a teacher with vision. Her challenge to us was to "reach for the stars." The crew of the *Challenger* would have wanted us to have a big vision. The best way we can honor them is to work hard and make our dreams come true.

Picture your dreams. Focus on a vision. What colors are your dreams? Draw a portrait of yourself with a background illustration to portray your vision—your lofty dreams.

Paint the portrait of your vision in your mind and heart. Mix the colors of your portrait with a brush of hope, a spark of imagination, and a stroke of enthusiasm on your easel of hard work. And watch your dreams come true.

CREATIVE ENCOUNTER #2 ....Snapshots of Time

"There is a tremendous value in the smallest daily events of our lives. Look at those as special gifts to treasure. Look on each day as a gift, and know the value of time and people. Know the value of time with people, helping people. Money is unlimited, but time is very limited."

Rediscover the importance of small things. The simple things in life are the essence of life. Relish the childlike joys of everyday wonders. When was the last time you were touched by wonder? Have you taken a moment to listen to a robin's song, watch a sunset, or say a kind word? Can you find joy in a snapshot of time or a thimbleful of fun?

A Day in the Life of America is a scrapbook of a nation. On May 2, 1986, two hundred leading photojournalists from twenty-seven countries captured America on film in the course of a day. Their assignment was to make extraordinary pictures of ordinary events.

Let's try to carry out that assignment. Pantomime an ordinary event. Hold that pose. Smile. Change the pose. How can you make an ordinary event extraordinary? Pantomime other daily events with background music to create an extraordinary touch.

What is extraordinary about your ordinary events in the course of a day? What simple things in life do you enjoy?

Capture those precious moments on three-dimensional film. Change the black and white film of a one-dimensional life-style to a color film of a multi-dimensional life-style. Boredom cannot enter the picture when you find enjoyment in the little things in life.

Your musical snapshots of small daily events play to a colorful tune. Listen to the whole notes of family time and quarter notes of friendship time, interspersed with staccato notes of fun time. Hearing that song can help you through the ups and downs of everyday living. Store the musical snapshots of time in a mental scrapbook of special memories.

CREATIVE ENCOUNTER #3 ....A Servant Leader

"I would like the students to know Dick Scobee. I would like to tell them that he was a man, a modest man, a trusting friend, a private man who loved his family dearly, and who contributed mightily to his country's air and space effort."

Astronaut Dick Scobee was truly a servant leader. He dedicated his life to serve, and he led our country to new heights in our space program. A servant leader is an amazing paradox, isn't it? How can one be a servant and a leader? A servant leader is a servant first—someone who has chosen to give his/her time and talents to others.

Let's draw a profile of a servant leader. A servant leader serves with a commitment to a purpose and a vision. A servant leader leads with compassion, joy, and competence. A servant leader accepts others and helps them grow. A servant leader is constructively involved with people. A servant leader sacrifices through service. A servant leader is an encourager. A servant leader is a creative problem solver. A servant leader can be a good follower.

In contrast, let's draw a profile of a limousine leader. A limousine leader seeks prominence through dominance. A limousine leader drives with tunnel vision. A limousine leader stops exploring. A limousine leader drives others to exhaustion with heavy demands. A limousine leader walks on people to make it to the top. A limousine leader does not stop to praise, but thrusts forth with destructive criticism. A limousine leader seizes all the recognition.

Contrast other characteristics of a servant leader with a limousine leader. List several leaders throughout history (George Washington, Adolf Hitler). Discuss their leadership styles, and classify each as a servant leader or a limousine leader.

Put yourself in the driver's seat, and evaluate your own leadership abilities. In what ways can you develop your leadership skills? Specify what you plan to do to become a servant leader. How will you drive on the road of life to reach your leadership potential?

CREATIVE ENCOUNTER #4 . . . . Flying High with Risks

"Everywhere I go, I'm asked if I'll tell children about risks . . . To risk is to grow, for without risks, there can be no new knowledge, no new discovery, no technological advancement, no bold adventure—all of which help the human spirit to soar. Who among you would argue that the greatest risk is to take no risk at all? Dick Scobee said, 'If you find something you really enjoy and the risks are worth it, you probably ought to take the risk.' "

Bring new adventure and exuberance to your life by daring to risk. Take a giant leap. Let's explore what risk entails.

To be vulnerable is to risk being misunderstood.

To love is to risk rejection.

To be gentle is to risk being crushed.

To dream big is to risk broken dreams.

To _____ is to risk _____ .

To _____ is to risk _____ .

To _____ is to risk _____ .

June says the challenge is worth the risks. Someone who does not take these risks may avoid suffering but cannot grow or change; the rewards and excitement of new ventures will be missed.

List examples of calculated risks and foolhardy risks, and contrast them on the back of this page. These could be mental, physical, or emotional risks. For example, a bicyclist needs self-discipline and training to risk competing in a bicycle race. It is dangerous to enter a bicycle race without calculated preparation.

Also, list jobs that involve risks. What makes these jobs risky? Farmers take risks. Their hard labor can be destroyed in one tempestuous storm.

What new adventures will you seek? Write the risks you dare to take in hot air balloons (playing a silly character in a skit, standing alone for what is right in a crowd).

Risk enlarges our horizons. Fly to new horizons by daring to risk. Boredom cannot enter your flight when you take risks. Fuel that adventurous spirit with courage and soar above the clouds. Up, up and away . . . !

128

CREATIVE ENCOUNTER #5 . . . . A View of Strength

Imagine looking down at Earth in a space shuttle. From space we can see all the majesty and power of Earth. Poverty-stricken conditions, crime, and conflict between nations are far removed. Feast upon the magnificent sunrise and sunset and the colorful blending of the countries and continents in this spectacular view.

Just as Earth is seen in a different perspective from the view of a space shuttle, let's focus on a new telescopic view of strength. Strengthen your grip on the meaning of strength. Look through the window and envision pillars of strength. Obviously, we see strength in athletic prowess, the independent spirit, and triumphant victories. But look closely now, and focus on a different view.

See the pillars of strength in tears. A drawback in our society is its reluctance to show tears. Tears are often considered a sign of weakness, of immaturity. Therefore, the curtain of restraint is closed upon hearts. The result is a well-guarded, uninvolved heart. Tears can spring upon us when others look to us for strength. Teardrops can water the garden of friendship, mend a broken relationship, or embrace the weak. Tears have a language all their own. Listen to their cry of sorrow or their whisper of joy.

Gaze at the mighty pillars of strength in an ability to express love toward others. See the strength in a willingness to depend upon others. When you let other people know your needs, it can show strength, not weakness. It gives them the satisfaction of using their gifts and service to help you.

Pillars of strength are built within us as we advance through adversity. Strength is seen in a leader who serves. See the towers of strength in gentleness and meekness.

Draw a powerful picture of strength in your mind. What are other ways you see strength? Think of specific incidents where strength is manifested. How is strength portrayed in a person who is struck down physically? When can strength be a weakness? When can a weakness be strength? How has your concept of strength changed? What pillars of strength are building in you?

How can you give strength to others? How can you be a people helper? What can you say when you don't know what to say? Talk about guidelines in developing your people-helping skills.

CREATIVE ENCOUNTER #6 . . . . Advancing Through Adversity

"It is our pioneers who take the risk and pay the price for what they believe in. Astronauts as well as teachers are pioneers who take risks and forge the way for others to follow. Those of you who are the pioneers will provide the leadership."

Suffering is the basis of good leadership. That's another paradox, isn't it? Out of pain comes leadership. Adversity shapes a leader into a trophy of proven character.

Let's look to nature to illustrate this point. Pearls are products of pain. A grain of sand or some other foreign substance finds its way inside the shell of the oyster. This irritates the sensitive oyster. All the resources within the oyster rush to the spot and begin to release healing fluids that otherwise would have remained dormant. Eventually the irritant is covered, and the wound is healed by a pearl. A gem is born of adversity.

Pain is inevitable. Living a life of misery is optional. How will you respond to the sands of adversity that pierce your life? You have a choice. Adversity can make you bitter, resentful, and harsh, or it can teach you valuable lessons. Are you willing to advance through adversity? Make the pearl of adjustment, and adversity can fashion you into a rare, precious jewel. Your inner character will shine with priceless, attractive qualities.

What are other illustrations from nature that can teach us lessons about advancing through adversity? Kites rise against the wind, not with the wind. Like the wind against a kite, adversity can lift us higher.

What pioneers throughout history have displayed courage as they advanced through adversity? What price have they paid for what they believe in? Design a banner of courage in honor of a pioneer. Create a Hall of Fame for these heroes. You and your classmates can draw a series of illustrations on a mural to depict each of these brave people and their beliefs.

INDEPENDENT PROJECTS—SCOBEE

1. *"There's a tremendous enthusiasm in young children, and they want to look to the future with hope. I've received thousands of letters from youngsters all over the nation. They tell me not to hide myself in a closet, to work hard and keep building programs for youth and to work with the Challenger Center."* Become a "studentnaut," and write a positive scenario about the future of the space program.
2. After Dick Scobee's first shuttle mission in 1984, June and Dick went out to dinner. While at the table, Dick kept tucking his napkin under his plate. He was trying to keep the napkin from floating away and didn't realize it. Build a space station of information about the astronauts' training, duties, and life in a spacecraft.
3. America watched in suspense, as 18-month-old Jessica McClure was rescued from the bottom of an abandoned well in a Texas town in October, 1987. The fifty-eight-hour ordeal ended with cheers and tears. Stuffed animals, presents, and donations poured in. Think of an event in history when America united in spirit to come to the aid of people in need. Draw an illustration of a music box, and choose an appropriate song to depict this event.
4. Search for the heroes behind heroes. Choose two or more of your heroes, and find out about the people who were the "building blocks" behind your heroes.
5. Become one of your heroes. Dress up and tell about your true adventures. Add background music and sound effects to embellish your soliloquy.
6. Confronting someone is a risk. Together caring and confronting can provide the balance needed when a confrontation occurs. Discuss creative ways to solve conflict. What communication skills can be implemented to turn confronting into care-fronting?

RESOURCE BOOKS—SCOBEE

Augsburger, David. new rev. ed. *Caring Enough to Confront*. Ventura, California: Regal Books, 1981.

Bernstein, Joanne E. *Books to Help Children Cope with Separation and Loss*. New York: R.R. Bowker Co., 1977.

Billings, Charlene W. *Christa McAuliffe: Pioneer Space Teacher*. Hillside, New Jersey: Enslow Publishers, Inc., 1986.

Briggs, Lauren. *What You Can Say . . . When You Don't Know What to Say*. Eugene, Oregon: Harvest House Publishers, 1985.

Cohen, Daniel, and Susan Cohen. *Heroes of the Challenger*. New York: Pocket Books, 1986.

Hohler, Robert T. *"I Touch the Future . . ." The Story of Christa McAuliffe*. New York: Random House, Inc., 1986.

Kent, Zachary. *The Story of the Challenger Disaster*. Chicago: Childrens Press, 1986.

Kerrod, Robin. *The Illustrated History of NASA*. New York: Gallery Books, 1986.

Marshall, Peter, and David Manuel. *The Light and the Glory*. Old Tappan, New Jersey: Fleming H. Revell Co., 1977.

The Staff of the *Washington Post. Challengers: The Inspiring Life Stories of the Seven Brave Astronauts of Shuttle Mission 51-L*. New York: Pocket Books, 1986.

Wright, H. Norman. *How to Have a Creative Crisis*. Waco, Texas: Word Books, 1986.

Yenne, Bill. *The Astronauts: The First 25 Years of Manned Space Flight*. New York: Exeter Books, 1986.

WALK FROM DARKNESS TO LIGHT

TOM SULLIVAN

"We blind, we handicapped, have an inconvenience, often a great inconvenience, but this inconvenience doesn't have to be a weakness. It can be our strength and, paradoxically, it can give strength to others.

"It is not the world that has to adjust to us. It is we who have to adjust to the world. We are live, viable creatures. We are people. There is not one of us who cannot do some job and do it well. The hard task is to begin, but once you've made a start, keep going and your world will suddenly expand in excitement and challenge. You will astound and delight your families. You will elate yourselves. And once you have learned to walk, you can begin to run.

"You are special; believe it. You are special; celebrate it. Learn to love and appreciate your specialness, for you are, indeed, special."

Tom Sullivan

BIOGRAPHICAL SKETCH

Tom was born three months too early and weighed only three pounds. In the hospital in West Roxbury, Massachusetts, he was placed in a newly invented incubator and given too much oxygen which resulted in his blindness. The happiest memories he has of his first two or three years are the stories told to him by his grandmother. Those days of his early childhood were lonely ones, because he had few friends, and he was isolated in a fenced yard and overprotected. He met his first friends, who wanted to join in, when they saw Tom and his father playing games. His father devised a basket with a buzzer so that he became almost as accurate at shooting a basketball as his sighted peers—indeed, more accurate at twilight. At the age of nine Tom's father surprised him when he brought home a tandam bicycle. He grew to love animals and had several pets.

Tom constantly searched about for ways to enter the world of the nonhandicapped. At the age of fourteen he wedged his foot in the door to the sighted world through wrestling. He won in 384 consecutive wrestling matches—a record that led him to a U.S. national title and an invitation to participate in the Olympic trials. Tom enjoys horseback riding, boating, jogging, and swimming. When he water-skis, the driver of the boat signals him with a bicycle horn.

Educated at the Perkins School for the Blind, Providence College, and Harvard University, his talents drew him in many directions. Tom is a musician, sportsman, actor, lecturer, and best-selling author. He is a marathon runner, 20-handicap golfer, excellent skier, world class competitor in wrestling with over 150 match victories. Tom has performed in live concerts throughout the world. He was invited to sing the National Anthem at the 1976 Super Bowl in Miami. Tom composed and performed the music for his biographical film, *If You Could See What I Hear.* He has made appearances on television programs and has been in films. Over two hundred colleges and hundreds of American corporations have been motivated and touched by Tom's person-to-person speaking style.

Tom lives with his wife, Patty, and their two children, Blythe and Tommy, in Palos Verdes, California, and works to share an ongoing closeness that he says means more than any of the rest of his accomplishments. Tom relishes and celebrates all aspects of life. His blindness has allowed him to turn disadvantage into advantage and give something unique and special to this world.

CREATIVE ENCOUNTER #1 . . . . A Radio Serial

"I have a sort of built-in television screen inside my brain, as do most people. I loved the radio serials, especially the westerns. I would tune in my BTV (brain television) and imitate the sounds.

"For instance, I discovered that bottle caps made a noise just like the jingle of spurs, and I found a way of tapping my slippers on the floor so that they sounded like a galloping horse. Using two brass curtain rods, I could re-create the sound of men fighting a duel with swords. My world was full of make-believe."

Divide into small groups, and make up a radio serial. Create a variety of sounds like Tom did and include commercials. Present it to a "radio audience." Tape-record it for future listening enjoyment.

CREATIVE ENCOUNTER #2 . . . . Following Directions

"I used up an immense amount of time simply getting from my dorm to class. Sometimes when I asked for help, the response might be, 'Sorry, but I'm going to have to run. Just turn right at the mailbox on that corner, and then take a left when you reach the yellow building.'

"In trying to follow fatuous directions like this I would find myself completely lost. When endeavoring to make up time I often had savage collisions with parked cars, street lamps or other solid objects which bruised and battered me from head to shin."

Think carefully and give very explicit directions, as if you were giving them to a blind person. Ask your partner to follow your directions, and evaluate your conciseness. Change roles.

CREATIVE ENCOUNTER #3 . . . . A Potpourri of Senses

As your teacher reads the imaginative journey, visualize yourself in Tom's world of darkness. After your journey, discuss this question. If you could see what Tom hears, what would you see?

Let's walk in the footsteps of Tom. Close your eyes. Walk from light into darkness. Enter a world of adventures in darkness. Use your vivid imagination and discover a potpourri of senses.

Commune with nature with all your senses. The sounds of birds, the smell of flowers, the touch of autumn leaves, and the taste of coming rain have become like old friends to you. Listen to the waves at the sea. Hear a trillion drops of water all playing their own tune. Take a big breath of air and taste the ocean as the rhythm of your feet dig footprints along untracked sand. Notice the unique patterns of seashells.

Pick up a pinecone and feel all those little depressions and points that are quite different. Listen to the snowflakes fall. Taste a snowflake. Smell the cold winter air. Enjoy a fire, crackling on a winter's day, when you are warmed by its warmth, soothed by its sound, comforted by its smell.

Touch the ground—the wonder of the ground on the first day of spring when the earth seems moist and promising. Smell a wet-with-dew rose just before it opens and a lilac in full bloom. Take in with all your senses a velvet blanket of wildflowers spread across a meadow. Listen to the animals. They seem to sense your presence. View a sunset, which is like taking a thousand pieces of glass of different shapes and letting them fall to form their own patterns. A sunset is like closing the day with happiness.

Celebrate life. Listen to the sound of a smile. See the color of laughter and taste the wonder of joy. Reach out of darkness for life. Open your eyes to what courage and life are all about. Journey from sightlessness to new insights. Walk from darkness into light.

CREATIVE ENCOUNTER #4 ....Skydive to New Dimensions

"Little Tommy's eyes are fresh windows on my world. He tells me about many things I cannot see. I tell him how to use his senses of touch, smell, taste and hearing. So my little son is also discovering a world that is so much more fascinating than the world that is only seen."

Tom added another dimension to his life when he learned to skydive. Imagine you are skydiving in slow motion. Your eyes are windows on the world. See the world in a new perspective. Open the windows to discover a fascinating world. Explore new dimensions in using all your senses.

Develop your skills in flexibility by responding to these questions. For example, what is the sound of freedom like? The sound of an American flag whipping in the wind? Draw a large window on another sheet of paper. Illustrate several of your responses in the window to create a potpourri of senses. Use fabrics, feathers, and other materials to create a three-dimensional effect.

What is the texture of friendship like? _____

What is the weight of adversity like? _____

What is the taste of joy like? _____

What is the sound of anger like? _____

What is the color of Saturday? _____

What is the sound of a snowflake like? _____

What is the color of a song? _____

What is the smell of a cloud like? _____

What is the sound of skydiving like? _____

What is the smell of sunshine like? _____

What is the color of blindness? _____

What is the sound of deafness like? _____

What is the color of apathy? _____

What is the weight of depression like? _____

What is the taste of tears like? _____

What is the texture of home like? _____

What is the sound of a smile like? _____

CREATIVE ENCOUNTER #5 ....Turn Adversity into Advantage

"All of us must learn how to turn adversity into advantage. I decided that out of adversity can come strength."

Tom was in the middle of the ninth inning in one of his make-believe games when a little boy came by his fence. He looked through the fence, and he saw Tom carrying out his make-believe game and said, *"How you doing, Blindey?"*

Now Tom realizes that the little boy was just curious and wasn't really ridiculing him. He only knew Tom by his label, "Blindey."

Imagine that you knew Tom when he was a child. You see that he is upset because he was called "Blindey." Tom has often been misunderstood because of his blindness. Role-play a conversation between Tom and his friends, who are encouraging Tom to turn adversity into advantage.

CREATIVE ENCOUNTER #6 ....Animal Partners

"Heidi did what she was trained to do and did it gallantly. But she more than saved my life. She helped to change my life at the deepest level. She helped me understand that we are, each one of us, our brother's keeper. I had first to recognize that if an animal, a dog, is ready to sacrifice its life for a human body, how much more responsible is every human being for his fellow man."

Heidi, a German shepherd, was Tom's eyes. When a car swerved around the corner, Heidi leaped at his chest and threw him backward. The car struck Heidi. Heidi's wound was not fatal, although she took many painful weeks to recover from the accident.

Trained animals are partners to the disabled. In therapeutic equitation programs, many people with disabilities can have the exercise and pleasure of riding with the help of professional instructors and specially trained horses. A dog named Skeezer that lived in a children's mental hospital helped many frightened, disturbed children. She was never too busy to listen to a child's secrets. Dogs are trained to aid the deaf and the blind. There are programs that provide the elderly in nursing homes with pets.

Read true stories about animals that have helped people. Make a booklet of the animal partners with illustrations.

Listen to the animals. Find unusual facts about animals. Usually dolphins travel as families. When one is injured, the family will push their kin to the top of the water so the dolphin can breathe. Dolphins care about each other and help each other, which is a good reminder for people. What other lessons for living can we learn from animals?

CREATIVE ENCOUNTER #7 ....The Magic of Seeing

"We take our eyes for granted so often and use them just to keep from bumping into things. We do a lot of looking every day: through lenses, telescopes, television tubes. We look more and more, but see less and less. Unless we slow down to see more than just labels and directions, we become merely spectators," states Tim Hansel in *When I Relax I Feel Guilty.*

Tim suggests the following to discover the magic of seeing. See color, for example. Follow one color for the whole day. You will be amazed at how much you've been blind to.

Sit quietly on the grass and allow your eyes to marvel at the world around you. A bush, a cloud, or a leaf might become an unforgettable experience. Draw a circle about six feet in diameter around you and see as many things as you can within that "magic circle." Take a pencil and sketch pad, and explore your artistic talents.

"People with sight cannot look at anyone or anything for long without losing concentration. It's the other way around for me. My concentration builds up when I meet someone. My senses distill an essence. I'm not distracted by movement. I zero in on people and stay with them. Sight paints a picture of life, but sound, touch, taste and smell are actually life itself."

Tom's eyes may not see, but his heart does. With the eyes of the heart we can look beyond a person's handicap and see the inner beauty. Cultivate the gift of insight. Open the eyes of your heart. Open your eyes and ears, and see and listen with your heart. Look beyond a smile and see if that person is really hurting on the inside. Look beyond a mask of superficiality, and try to get to know a person on a deeper level. Look beyond a handicap, and see a person ready to love and be loved.

Imagine what it would be like to pick up a book to enjoy, only to find that you cannot read it, because the page is entirely blank except for bumps. Or suppose you entered a room where everyone was speaking in sign language, and you couldn't join in.

Many handicapped people feel just this sense of frustration when they try to participate in activities with people without handicaps. We have much to learn from these people, as well as much to give them. Below are some activities to help you to see beyond—to put yourself in their place. The following are based on experiments by Ruth Shuman, who is blind. She is the founder of an organization in Chicago to help educate people to relate to the handicapped.

Have someone string a group of objects on a line. Put on a blindfold, and try to identify the items by touch alone. What were your thoughts as you moved, unseeing, from object to object?

Still blindfolded, practice walking around the room using a sighted person as a guide or using a cane. Discuss how it felt and what new things you discovered.

Make a collection of small items, such as safety pins, buttons, paper clips, sequins, and coins. Try picking them up one at a time while wearing rubber gloves. How did this exercise help you understand the arthritic person or other handicapped people who have difficulty using their hands?

To empathize with those who have cerebral palsy or dyslexia, try this. Stand a mirror at right angles with a tabletop. Place a piece of paper on the tabletop directly in front of the mirror. Now, by looking at the paper only in the mirror, try to write your name so it can be read correctly looking in the mirror. Remember, don't look at the paper, just look in the mirror. When you've finished, you can look directly at the paper, where your name will appear backward.

Try understanding the deaf or the hard of hearing. Spend a half an hour or so watching television with the sound turned off. Next, try communicating to someone about the program, but use only your hands, facial expressions, or sign language. No talking allowed. Were you able to communicate your message?

Watch television blindfolded. Sharpen your imagination, and try to vividly see the colors and action. Still blindfolded, communciate what you visualized to someone using a variety of action words and adjectives.

"Don't be afraid to ask me if I need any help. When you speak to me, ask me things instead of addressing your questions to my companion. One of the most important attitudes is friendliness," suggests Ruth Shuman. Make a chart of other helpful suggestions on how to relate to the handicapped.

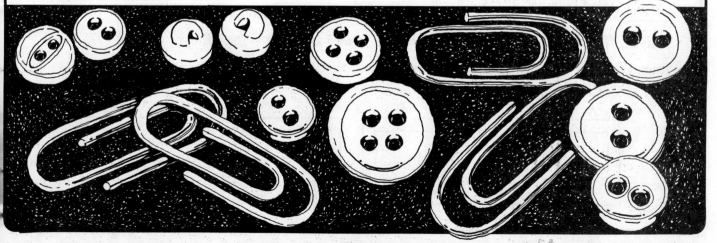

135

INDEPENDENT PROJECTS—SULLIVAN

1. *"There are many interesting games you can play with your friends to test their ability to 'see' with their ears, their noses, and their fingers. For instance, on a tape recorder you can record familiar sounds, like the shwoosh of brushing teeth, the striking of a match, the whirr of a vacuum cleaner, and the flutter of thumbing your fingers through the pages of a book. Then find out how many of your friends can guess what these sounds are."*

2. Many people ask Ruth Shuman how she does everyday activities blind. Here are some of her blindfold experiments. Walk around your house blindfolded. Identify objects, such as toys, furniture, and clothes by touch. Eat a meal blindfolded. You can put your food on the plate like a clock—meat at 12:00, vegetables at 3:00, etc. Try to shoot a basketball, etc., with one hand. Do other safe experiments with a friend to limit each one of your senses. This will help you develop your senses to a higher degree. Report back to your class what you learned from limiting your senses.

3. Open your eyes and heart; open them wide. Gain insight into the minds and hearts of the handicapped. Imagine that you know your sight and hearing are irretrievably lost. Give an oral presentation for your class of what you think life would be like being blind or deaf or living with another handicap. Use props, such as a cane. Try to give your talk from the point of view of a handicapped person.

4. Research careers that involve training or using animals to help handicapped people.

RESOURCE BOOKS—SULLIVAN

Curtis, Patricia. *Animal Partners: Training Animals to Help People.* New York: E.P. Dutton, Inc., 1982.

Gill, Derek L.T. *Tom Sullivan's Adventures in Darkness.* New York: David McKay Co., Inc., 1976.

Haskins, James. *Who Are the Handicapped?* Garden City, New York: Doubleday & Co., Inc., 1978.

Hayman, LeRoy. *Triumph!: Conquering Your Physical Disability.* New York: Julian Messner, 1982.

Holzhauser, Gillian K. *Making the Best of It: How to Cope with Being Handicapped.* New York: Ballantine Books, 1986.

Kay, Jane G. *Crafts for the Very Disabled and Handicapped for All Ages.* Springfield, Illinois: Charles C. Thomas, 1977.

Montanus, Ralph, and Harold Hostetler. *That They Might See.* Nashville, Tennessee: Thomas Nelson, Inc., 1985.

Schattner, Regina. *Creative Dramatics for Handicapped Children.* New York: The John Day Co., 1967.

Sullivan, Tom. *Common Senses.* Nashville, Tennessee: Ideals Publishing Corporation, 1982.

_____. *You Are Special.* Nashville, Tennessee: Ideals Publishing Corporation, 1980.

Sullivan, Tom, and Derek Gill. *If You Could See What I Hear.* New York: Harper & Row, 1975.

Yates, Elizabeth. *Skeezer: Dog with a Mission.* New York: Harvey House, Inc., 1973.

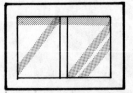   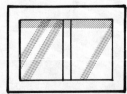